Praise for *Let's Make a Contract*

Let's Make a Contract absolutely inspired me. The day after reading it, I made some changes in my parenting approach and had a wonderful day with my nonverbal son, following a handful of really tough days. The concepts are explained in plain language, and the scenarios are so relatable for any parent. I highly recommend this book for parents of neurodiverse and neurotypical kids.

Lorri Unumb, CEO, Council of Autism Service Providers

If 30 years of working with children and families have taught me anything, it's that parents who respect their children's views and use their input, especially regarding the clarity of parental expectations and the fairness of rewards/recognitions for meeting them, have happier families. There are many ways to achieve this and one of the most powerful and efficient is the behavioral contract. For a clear, easy to understand (and implement) guide, look no further than this delightful book by two universally respected veterans of the child and family field.

Patrick C. Friman, Ph.D., ABPP, Vice President of Behavioral Health, Boys Town

Let's Make a Contract is a thorough and engaging guide for helping any family turn a negative behavioral situation into a positive one through contracting. This book clearly outlines steps for developing effective contracts and gives practical examples to identify potential pitfalls, so that the contract can be successfully implemented. Lots of practical examples, illustrations, and sample contracts make what could be a complex topic easy to read and follow.

Lynn Kern Koegel, Ph.D., Professor, Stanford School of Medicine; Coauthor, *Overcoming Autism and Growing Up on the Spectrum*; Recipient, Children's Television Workshop Sesame Street Award

This book touches my heart. With tenderness and respect, Drs. Dardig and Heward invite families to embark on a journey of intentional and shared growth. They provide important and practical guidance to help parents and children navigate possible actions, expectations, and consequences. Above all, they model the clarity, affection, and responsibility that characterizes the best of behavior change programs.

Shahla Ala'i-Rosales, Ph.D., BCBA-D,
Family Harmony Researcher, University of North Texas

Wow, Jill Dardig and Bill Heward have crafted a terrific resource for parents, grandparents, aunts, uncles, and anyone else who spends time with kids. Through humorous, realistic vignettes, *Let's Make a Contract* shares a time-tested strategy—contracting—for promoting positive behavior, shared responsibility, and a bit of self-management. Whether it be academic behaviors, household chores, or personal goals, *Let's Make a Contract* is bound to get you and your kids excited about getting things done.

Janet S. Twyman, Ph.D., BCBA, LBA,
Founder, blast (A Learning Sciences Company)

In a captivating story-telling style, Jill Dardig and Bill Heward have masterfully crafted practical guidelines for developing and implementing behavioral contracts. In their hands, this technique—which is solidly grounded on scientific principles—becomes a fun learning opportunity for any family member to succeed at changing a behavior or attaining a personal goal. While this wonderful resource is intended for parents, it's equally useful for other caregivers and professionals who want a proven, positive approach to behavior change.

Amiris Dipuglia, MD, BCBA, Educational/Parent Consultant,
Pennsylvania Training and Technical Assistance Network

If you are a parent, read this book today. Humorous vignettes bring to life a straightforward roadmap for how to establish healthy communication, goal setting, and positive behavior in all family members. Dr. Dardig and Dr. Heward transform research-based procedures into positive parenting tools for raising children who take responsibility for their own behavior. An earlier version of this book remains in print in an astounding 10 languages. While the examples in *Let's Make a Contract* are thoroughly modernized, the principles are the same that have helped parents succeed for more than 45 years.

Bridget A. Taylor, PsyD., BCBA-D,
Co-founder and CEO of Alpine Learning Group

Let's Make a Contract is an example of the best that the science of behavior has to offer families. The authors provide practical and positive guidance to parents and caregivers on what to do when a child is struggling with behavior. The variety of family dynamics and issues that the book covers provide an abundance of relevant—and realistic—information.

Fernando Armendariz, Ph.D., BCBA-D, Director, FABAS

In *Let's Make a Contract*, Jill Dardig and Bill Heward do an amazing job of presenting a step-by-step approach to help parents and children improve their lives through contracts. The stories and sample forms make it easy for parents (and professionals) to create and adapt contracts for children of any age or ability level.

Mary Lynch Barbera, Ph.D., RN, BCBA-D,
Best-Selling Author, *Turn Autism Around*

In this fine book, there is a consistent invitation to see the world through the eyes of each family member, and by doing so, develop a greater understanding of each other and create a plan to improve the life of the family as a whole.

Darnell Lattal, Ph.D., CEO ABA Technologies

I wholeheartedly recommend this much-needed book that showcases the journey of families using contracts to address a diverse array of behaviors. Well-illustrated and narrated, the authors' insights, experiences, and compassion shine through. This clever book will be helpful to both parents and professionals alike.

David Celiberti, Ph.D., BCBA-D, Executive Director, Association for Science in Autism Treatment

Practical and without unnecessary jargon, *Let's Make a Contract* focuses on building positive relationships between children and their parents, rather than simply trying to stop bad behavior or build compliance. The clarity of the writing and the use of common examples of stressors in family life make this book a wonderful resource. I highly recommend this book to parents, educators, and anyone who wants to improve the quality of relationships among family members.

Robert K. Ross, Ed.D., BCBA-D, LABA, Chief Clinical Officer, Beacon ABA Services of Massachusetts and Connecticut

As a special education teacher and a parent of a child with a disability, I have found that managing behaviors in children and young adults is possible with the right tools. *Let's Make a Contract* is in that must-have category. I put the step-by-step directions to the test by creating a contract with my classroom students when we implemented virtual learning. My students clearly understanding the expectations and rewards based on the contract heavily contributed to making our virtual learning a success.

Danielle M. Kovach, Ed.D., President, Council for Exceptional Children

Let's Make a Contract

ISBN: 978-1-951412-51-7
Ebook ISBN: 978-1-951412-71-5
LCCN: 2021911392

Printed using Forest Stewardship Council certified stock
from sustainably managed forests.

Manufactured in China

Editing by Elizabeth Dougherty
Design by David Miles
Illustrations by Albert Pinilla

1 3 5 7 9 10 8 6 4 2

The Collective Book Studio
Oakland, California
www.thecollectivebook.studio

Let's Make a Contract

A Positive Way to Change Your Child's Behavior

JILL C. DARDIG   **WILLIAM L. HEWARD**

Elizabeth Dougherty, Editor   •   Albert Pinilla, Illustrator

Table of Contents

Foreword: Parenting . . . One of Life's Hardest Jobs,
  by Catherine Maurice 10

Preface: The Global Power of Stories 13

Introduction: Contracting and How to Use This Book 16

Part I: Read Together

1. Game Suspended 23

2. Loopholes 37

3. The Number Problem 49

4. The Pet Menace 59

5. Lynn Pitches In 71

6. By Myself 77

7. Siblings United 85

8. Now It's Your Turn, Mom and Dad 91

9. Making Friends... 99

Part II: Make Your Own Contracts

10. What Is Contracting?... 109

11. Select the Task.. 121

12. Choose the Reward 137

13. Write the Contract 147

14. Implement the Contract 163

15. Picture Contracts for Nonreaders 175

16. If Your Child Won't Try Contracting 185

Glossary 190

Resources 192

References 195

Acknowledgments 198

Contract Forms 200

Translations 208

Parenting . . . One of Life's Hardest Jobs

The concept might seem a bit odd at first: a contracting book for children and their parents? But, for any family who may be facing a persistent behavior problem that they don't know how to handle (and wouldn't that be all of us at some point during the course of raising our kids?), I highly recommend this book.

First of all, the authors offer a practical and research-backed approach to helping a child overcome dysfunctional behaviors that interfere not only with family peace and harmony but also with the child's own well-being. If you have a toddler who regularly throws tantrums to get his way or a preteen who neglects homework because she is becoming addicted to social media, it's helpful to have some time-tested and effective advice for dealing with those and many other challenging situations.

The two "advisers" in this case are Jill Dardig and Bill Heward, colleagues with whom I have collaborated on several publications, and people I am privileged to call friends. Both have accrued decades of knowledge and experience in education, special education, and behavior analysis, and both have dedicated their professional lives to helping families and children. On a personal level, I find them to be humble and giving people, not involved in this work for personal glory or fame or wealth (is there any "wealth" in special ed?) but singularly focused on bringing effective strategies to struggling parents and kids.

No one book and no parent has the perfect answer to one of life's hardest jobs—raising happy and productive children—but this book contains some very useful and helpful guidelines as we struggle to get it right.

The main strategy outlined here is to create a written contract between parents and child, between siblings if they so choose, or even a contract that a child makes with himself or herself. For nonreaders or very young children, a contract can be image-based, using drawings or photos instead of words.

Intrinsic to that organizing motif are several elements critical to the effectiveness of the intervention. One is the importance of setting clear expectations for children. Children will naturally gravitate toward behaving like children for better or for worse, unless someone clearly sets out for them what the expectations are for any given situation. How can they be expected to behave in church or at the dinner table unless someone has gently, kindly, and explicitly taught them what to do? It might happen sometimes, but it's mostly wishful thinking to assume that children will learn simply by osmosis or imitation. It helps the process enormously if there is a caring adult willing to set out the expectations beforehand.

The second critical element is then to reinforce or reward them when they do comply with those expectations. Applied behavior analysis has gotten a bad rap because people assume that it trains little ones in robotic compliance through a system of rewards and punishments, and yet, who among us would work if we did not get paid or get some kind of satisfaction, even altruistically, for our efforts? What would be the incentive to doing anything correctly or well unless there was some recompense or happiness to be found in doing so? Allowing children some form of reward for their efforts is not manipulative. It's common sense, and it's highly effective. Much more effective than harsh words and punishments. It doesn't even have to be something concrete. Children respond to words of praise, and they flourish when recognized for their efforts.

No one book and no parent has the perfect answer to one of life's hardest jobs—raising happy and productive children—but this book contains some very useful and helpful guidelines as we struggle to get it right.

–Catherine Maurice
Best-Selling Author, *Let Me Hear Your Voice,*
A Family's Triumph Over Autism

The Global Power of Stories

Early in our careers, we helped found an early intervention program for young children with disabilities in western Massachusetts. Most of the children served by the program were diagnosed with autism and exhibited severe behavioral challenges that created turmoil at home and at their previous schools, causing great stress for their parents. Bill was the program's lead teacher. Jill taught science-based behavior change principles and techniques to the parents through weekly group meetings and home visits, where she demonstrated what they were learning in class.

Jill was elated to find that most of the parents readily understood and applied the evidence-based principles with their children. Many of the parents had particular success using the tool of contracting. They told Jill contracts were easy to develop and both they and their kids liked having them.

Though happy about these positive outcomes, Jill was discouraged that she wasn't reaching a wider audience of parents, when the need for families to have positive, functional parenting tools is so great. Most parents don't receive any formal parent training. Jill wanted to find a way to give more families, especially those parents whose kids were not receiving support services but really needed them, access to these useful tools in a direct and cost-effective way. She wondered if a storybook could help families learn to use contracting on their own. Parents or older kids could read the stories themselves to understand how the process works, or they could read the stories to younger children to teach them how they could benefit. Bill loved this idea.

> If this book merely prompts family members to sit down and listen to each other's concerns and desires, we will consider it a great success.

As a result, we coauthored *Sign Here: A Contracting Book for Children and Their Parents*. First published in 1976, *Sign Here* used nontechnical language, humorous scenarios, and illustrations to tell how a family—two working parents and three kids—learns to use contracting to resolve problems and improve interactions.

We wrote an expanded second edition that was published in 1981, after three doctoral dissertation studies at The Ohio State University used *Sign Here* as the vehicle for teaching contracting in home and school settings and yielded positive results.

Sign Here has now been published in ten languages (see page 208) and is helping thousands of families around the world. The translators revised the stories to represent contemporary family life and cultural norms in their countries. The results have been inventive and inspiring. For example, the Chinese language edition is beautifully illustrated in full color, and the Japanese version is a creatively drawn manga comic.

In this new book, *Let's Make a Contract,* we've updated and expanded the stories to include diverse families, including children with disabilities. We've also made the instructions for creating contracts easier to implement by breaking them down into four key steps: select the task, choose the reward, write the contract, and implement the contract.

Above all, we hope families will find contracting fun. And, if this book merely prompts family members to sit down and listen to each other's concerns and desires, we will consider it a great success.

—Jill C. Dardig and William L. Heward

Contracting and How to Use This Book

At its heart, a contract is a written agreement between two people who each promise to do something. For example, you might agree to buy a car or home for a certain price, and the seller agrees to accept that price. A signed contract records this exchange and makes it official.

In this book, we look at a different kind of contract, called a *behavior contract* (also known as a *contingency contract*), that focuses on changing behavior—yours as well as your child's—in a positive, nonpunitive way. The core parts of a behavior contract are a *task* your child promises to complete and a *reward* they will receive for completing that task.

Using behavior contracts is a simple-yet-powerful way for your child to partner in solving behavior problems and reaching personal goals. The evidence supporting contracting is sound. In addition to the three dissertations that helped inform and refine the contracting method described in our book *Sign Here* (see Preface), many research studies have demonstrated the efficacy of contracting with children in school, clinical, and home settings (see References).

While contracting has been shown to be a versatile and effective technique for improving the family atmosphere, it is not a cure-all nor the right intervention for every situation. An effective contract serves as a short-term motivational device to get family members moving toward more positive and cooperative relationships and interactions. Most contracts can be phased out as children begin experiencing the natural rewards for completing tasks and using newly learned skills.

Parents' Roadmap for Reading This Book

Let's take a closer look at the structure of the book and how you might want to approach reading it.

We've written *Let's Make a Contract* in two parts: the first contains nine children's stories, and the second is how-to content for parents.

You can read the children's stories in Part I (*Read Together*) first, and then read Part II *(Make Your Own Contracts)*.

Alternatively, proceed directly to Part II, which describes a step-by-step process for creating and implementing behavior contracts. Refer to the stories as they're mentioned, or wait and read them after you finish the how-to information.

Following is more detailed information about the content in each part.

PART I: READ TOGETHER (CHILDREN'S STORIES)

Nine children's stories illustrate how four families use contracts to achieve goals and solve various problems. The stories provide a mini-course on how to construct a variety of behavior contracts with kids. They also illustrate common problems with contracts that might arise and how to fix them.

The stories are interconnected but can be read alone or in any order. You may want to read one or more of the stories to, or with, your child. Older children may enjoy reading the illustrated stories independently.

The "Let's Talk" questions that follow each story are prompts to kick off discussions with your child.

PART II: MAKE YOUR OWN CONTRACTS (HOW-TO FOR PARENTS)

The second part of the book contains how-to information for parents. The first five chapters cover the basics of contracting and the steps you'll take to create a behavior contract:

- *What Is Contracting?*
- *Select the Task*
- *Choose the Reward*
- *Write the Contract*
- *Implement the Contract*

The final two chapters address special situations:

- *Picture Contracts for Nonreaders*
- *If Your Child Won't Try Contracting*

How the Stories Relate to the How-To Steps

The how-to chapters reference relevant stories. Here's a summary of how they tie together and the key learning takeaways.

- In "Game Suspended," Jeff (age 10) makes a contract to clean up his messy room. What you'll learn: How to construct a contract with its three main parts: task, reward, and task record.

- In "Loopholes," Jeff tests the limits of his room-cleaning contract and plays a joke on his family. What you'll learn: How to specify the details of a task so that everyone understands what it is—and that it's okay to change a contract that isn't working.

- In "The Number Problem," Perry (10) wants to do better in math. What you'll learn: How to make a self-contract to improve an academic skill—and selecting the right task for a successful outcome.

- In "The Pet Menace," Maya (4), who has autism, learns to be kind to pets. What you'll learn: How to make a contract in pictures for a nonreader—and how to structure a reward so it is effective.

- In "Lynn Pitches In," Lynn's (14) parents work and need her to start dinner after school. What you'll learn: How to make a contract for a household chore.

- In "By Myself," Connor (10), who has autism, is having trouble getting ready on time for the school bus. What you'll learn:

How to make a contract that uses words and photos and has a checklist for a child to follow.

- In "Siblings United," Jeff and Lynn make a contract between themselves that benefits them both. What you'll learn: How siblings can make a contract.

- In "Now It's Your Turn, Mom and Dad," Jeff and Lynn make a contract with their parents to recognize their accomplishments and stop nagging them. What you'll learn: How parents can be the subjects of a behavior contract.

- In "Making Friends," Connor is unhappy that he doesn't have friends at school. His mom and behavior analyst meet with his teacher to help him learn how to make friends. What you'll learn: How to make a contract that teaches a social skill—and how to make a home/school contract.

We're delighted and excited to provide information and tools to help you in your all-important role as a parent. We wish you and your family positive and satisfying results with your contracts!

Companion Website

Contract forms and other resources to help you create your own contracts are available at contractingwithkids.com.

PART I

Read Together

1

Game Suspended

Jeff is supposed to be quiet after school when his dad sleeps before he goes to work at night, and his older sister, Lynn, is supposed to start dinner before their mom comes home from her job. Both kids know they're *supposed* to do these things, but they often *don't*.

Jeff and Perry splashed through the rain, running from school to Jeff's house. The two friends pounded up the stairs, threw open the door to Jeff's bedroom, banging the doorknob against the wall, and flopped on the floor to catch their breath.

"Since it's too wet to play outside, let's finish the game we started at recess," Perry said, picking up a small basketball.

"Bring it on!" Jeff yelled, jumping up and holding out his arms to try to block Perry's shot.

Perry bounced the ball on the wood floor a few times, took two giant steps, and threw the ball through the little hoop mounted on the wall. The boys both grabbed the ball and tumbled on the floor, holding on to it and laughing.

The fun ended when Jeff's dad, Joe, appeared at the bedroom doorway. He looked unhappy. He also looked tired.

"Jeff, what's going on?" his dad said. "You know I work at night and need to sleep during the day. Game over. We'll talk later."

Joe walked away, and Perry quickly left.

Jeff found his father shaving in the bathroom.

"Sorry, Dad. I didn't mean to wake you up. I forget to be quiet."

"Most people are lucky to have a daytime job," Joe said. "Me, I work at night. That means I have to sleep during the day. I don't like it any better than you do."

Jeff thought about how tired his dad looked when he came home in the morning as the rest of the family was just starting their day.

"I'll try not to do it again," Jeff said.

"You've been saying that all along, but you still keep waking me up. We're going to have to figure out something different that works."

Jeff really was sorry he'd woken up his dad, but it also made him sad his dad was mad at him.

Jeff's mom, Evelyn, came home from work. Jeff knew she was home because he could hear her yelling from the kitchen for his sister, Lynn, to get off her phone and start dinner.

"Hi, Mom," Jeff said as he popped into the kitchen. "How was your day?"

"It was okay until I came home to a messy house and saw that Lynn hadn't started dinner," Evelyn said. "Speaking of chores, have you fed the dog today and taken out the trash?"

"Jeff and his friend Perry woke me up again," Joe added as he came into the kitchen.

"Jeff, we don't ask you to do that many things, so why can't you do the few things we expect?" Evelyn asked.

Jeff felt like everyone was picking on him.

Woof-woof-woof. Now it was the dog's turn to complain. Tucker was sitting by his empty food bowl and barking. Jeff gave Tucker a scoop of food, which he gobbled up.

"Let's go, Tucker," Jeff said, grabbing the bag of garbage.

The dog followed him outside. Jeff threw away the trash while Tucker ran to fetch a ball for Jeff to throw. Tucker dropped a bright-yellow one at Jeff's feet. Jeff tossed the ball across the yard. Tucker raced after the ball, ran back to Jeff, and dropped the ball at Jeff's feet again. Tucker sat, wagging his tail.

"At least you're happy," Jeff said to the dog. "Everyone else in this family is always mad. I get in trouble every day."

Jeff picked up the ball and gave it another toss.

"When everyone is picking on each other like this, I wish I were someplace else, even at school," Jeff said.

Jeff played fetch with Tucker until his mom called him for dinner.

Things didn't get any better during the meal. Everyone was in a bad mood and complaining.

"Jeff and Lynn, I'm tired of asking you to pick up after yourselves," Evelyn said. "When I get home from work, a messy house is the last thing I want to see."

"If you have time to be on your phone, you have time to put your stuff away," their dad added.

"You're always bossing us around," Lynn said. "Do this! Do that!"

"I'm tired of everyone always being mad at each other," Jeff said.

Evelyn raised her hands for silence.

"Enough," she said. "Everyone stop talking and listen to me. We're all part of this family, and we have to work things out together. After dinner, we're going to have a family meeting. It's time we made some changes around here."

After they ate and everyone put their own dirty dishes in the dishwasher, they gathered back at the kitchen table.

"All right, everyone, this family meeting will now come to order," Joe said. "Everyone will have a chance to speak. I think that if you kids would do what you're supposed to do, everyone would be happier."

"Just to be clear about what we expect you to do," Evelyn said. "Jeff, when you come home from school, be quiet so your dad can sleep, clean up your room, feed the dog, and take out the trash."

"I mean to do that," Jeff said. "But after school all day, I want to have fun when I get home, and then I forget."

"You can have fun, but you need to do your chores first," Joe said. "It's not okay if you haven't done those things."

"Jeff's not the only one who doesn't do his share around here," Evelyn added. "Lynn, it seems like every day when I get home from work you're on your phone texting or playing a game."

"Mom," Lynn said, "even if I get dinner started before you get home, you still yell at me for being on my phone too much. It feels like we can't do anything right."

"All right, all right," Evelyn said. "Everyone is unhappy about something. We're a family, though, and we love each other, right? We can work together to make changes that are good for everyone."

"Yes, Mom," Jeff agreed.

"You're right, honey," Joe added.

"I've got an idea," Lynn said. "It might sound funny, but we do it in Ms. Jackson's language arts class, and it works great."

"What is it?" Joe asked. "If you have an idea you think will help, we want to hear it."

"Well, we make *contracts* with Ms. Jackson for completing various tasks," Lynn said. "It could be for turning in our homework on time or reading extra books."

"What do contracts have to do with our family?" Evelyn asked, confused.

"What's a contract?" Jeff asked.

"A contract is an agreement that says if you do something, you'll get something in return," Lynn said. "At school, if we complete a task our teacher asks us to do, she gives us a reward when we're done."

"I don't see why you need to have a contract to do what you're supposed to do anyway," Joe said. "Your mom and I never had contracts with our parents."

"That's true, Joe, but if contracts would get you kids to do what we ask you to do, maybe they are what we need," Evelyn said.

"Contracts also would say what *reward* you and Dad would give us when we finish the task we promise to do," Lynn said.

"A reward?" Joe asked. "You kids should be good without getting paid off. That's like paying you to do what you should do anyway."

"A reward doesn't have to be money," Lynn said. "The reward can be doing something fun together."

"I like that idea if it helps you kids be more responsible," Joe said. "Having more fun together could also help all of us get along better."

"Really? Can we try it?" Lynn asked.

"Yes, let's do it," Joe said.

"How do we make a contract?" Jeff asked.

"Contracts are usually written on a piece of paper," Lynn said. "When two people make a contract with each other, they both agree to everything the contract says."

"But what makes them do what's on the contract? How can a piece of paper make anybody do anything?" Jeff asked.

"When you finish the task on the contract, you get the reward on the contract," Lynn said. "In class, each time I finish a lesson in our online reading program, I get to read anything I want for ten minutes. I can even bring a magazine to school. But before you sign a contract, you must agree to *everything* it says. Contracts also have to be *fair* for everyone."

"So, I wouldn't write my name on a contract if I didn't think the reward was fair for what I said I'd do. Is that what you mean?" Jeff said.

"That's exactly right. There's also one more thing that helps make contracts work," Lynn said. "An official seal."

"What's that?" Jeff asked.

"An official seal is a personal stamp of approval," Lynn said. "It's like when the post office stamps 'priority mail' on a letter and guarantees that letter will arrive on a certain day. It makes that promise more formal. When we put our family's official seal on a contract, it reminds us that we need to be serious about doing what we promised to do."

"So what's our official seal?" Jeff asked.

"That's one of the fun things about contracts," Lynn said. "It's usually a small drawing, but it can be anything. Since you like to draw, you could make our family's official seal.

"Well, Mom and Dad," Lynn continued. "Since you're okay with trying contracts, I'll volunteer to have the first contract."

"I want a contract, too," Jeff said.

"Okay," Joe said. "No reason why you each can't have a contract."

"Mine will be about helping get dinner started," Lynn said.

"Mine will be for not waking up Dad when I get home from school," Jeff said.

"Why don't we all think about what we want our contracts to say," Evelyn said. "Tomorrow night, we can create them."

"And I'll make an official seal to put on our contracts to remind us that we're making a serious promise," Jeff said.

Jeff went to his room to draw an official seal. He pushed aside a stack of stuff on his desk, got out his colored pencils, and started to sketch some different ideas. It took a few tries before he figured out what he wanted to do. Then he set to work drawing a final copy.

The next morning, Jeff invited everyone to his room to see their family's own official seal. He had taped it to the wall with a plain piece of paper over it. While they all watched, Jeff took off the top piece of paper to reveal the seal, which was a drawing of the family's house.

"It's beautiful, Jeff," his mom said.

"Now *that's* a nice official seal," Lynn said.

"I like the seal, too," Joe said. "But I don't like how messy this room is."

Jeff looked around his room. He had to admit, it was really messy.

"You're right, Dad," Jeff said. "Maybe we should make my first contract about cleaning up my room instead of about being quiet."

"I think that's a great idea," Evelyn said. "Dad and I really don't like having to nag you constantly about cleaning up."

"Get some paper, Jeff. I'll show you how to make your first contract," Lynn said.

Somehow Jeff found a pen and a blank piece of paper under the mess on his desk.

"Okay," Lynn said. "On the left side of the paper, write what task you're going to do. On the right side, write the reward you'll get for doing the task."

Jeff wrote: "Task: Clean up bedroom."

"Mom and Dad, what should the reward be?" he asked.

"Well," his dad said, "how about this for a reward? If you clean up your room the whole week, I'll spend special time with you on Saturday. Just you and me."

"Really? That would be cool," Jeff said.

Jeff wrote: "Reward: Special time with Dad on Saturday."

Lynn explained that the final steps were adding their family's official seal and signing the contract.

Jeff drew the official seal on the contract. Then he and his dad signed it at the bottom.

"Well, we have a contract. Let's see how it works today," Joe said. "I'll be asleep when you get home from school. I look forward to seeing your room all clean when I wake up."

Let's Talk

- What problems are the family having?
- Why do they decide to try making contracts?
- Does your family have any problems you think a contract might help with?
- Do you think the contract Jeff and his dad made will work?

Contract

TASK	REWARD
Clean up bedroom	Special time with Dad on Saturday

sign here: *Jeff*

sign here: *Dad*

2

Loopholes

In "Game Suspended" Jeff got in trouble for waking up his dad and for not cleaning up his room. Jeff and his dad made a contract that said if Jeff cleaned up his room all week, they would spend special time together on Saturday. Here's what happened next.

Jeff ran all the way home from school. He wanted to get a head start on doing what he promised in his contract, which was to clean up his room. But he slowed down when he reached the house. He didn't want to be noisy and wake up his dad.

Cleaning up his room was easy. Jeff put his guitar back in its case, put his models and books on the shelf, made his bed, and put away his clothes. He worked fast, and it only took a few minutes to get it all done. He had to admit, his room looked good when it was neat. Jeff smiled as he headed to the dinner table.

After dinner, Jeff was excited to show off his clean room.

"Dad, come see how well I cleaned up my room, like I promised in our contract."

"Okay, okay, I'm coming," Joe said, following his son into the bedroom.

"Well, how did I do, Dad?" Jeff asked, happy with his clean room.

"It's a lot better, but your desk is still a mess," Joe said. "It needs to be clean before you can get credit for cleaning up your room."

"That's not fair. You didn't say anything about my desk being neat. The rest of the room looks great. I cleaned up my room, just like the contract says."

Jeff's voice was loud enough for his sister to hear from her bedroom.

"That's not the way I see it," Joe said. "If your desk is still messy, your room isn't clean."

"My room is clean!" Jeff insisted.

Lynn came into Jeff's room. "Since it was my idea to use contracts, maybe I can help."

"Contracts don't work," Jeff said.

"Your brother's right, Lynn," Joe added. "We wrote out a contract, and Jeff didn't fulfill his end of the bargain."

"I think a contract can still work," Lynn said. "It's just that I didn't tell you the most important rule about contracts. A contract must describe exactly what the task is. That way no one can argue later about whether or not the task was completed. That's the problem here."

"How do you know all this stuff?" Jeff asked.

"I told my teacher we were going to going to try making contracts at home, and she let me borrow this book." Lynn handed Jeff the book. "She said we could use it to help make our contracts. It's even got some forms we can copy to write our contracts.

"At first," she continued, "some of our contracts at school didn't work, and nobody liked them. Then our teacher had us make them more specific, and they worked a lot better."

"That makes sense," Joe said. "Jeff, let's write your contract again, using one of the examples in this book as a guide. It looks like adding a section about how well you're supposed to do the task will help us agree on exactly what it means to clean up your room."

Jeff and his dad talked about what Jeff had to do and came up with this list:

- Pick up all clothes off floor, bed, desk, and chair.

- Put guitar in case and models and books on shelves.

- Clear top of desk. Put pencils in mug on desk and homework in backpack.

- Make bed.

Then Jeff copied a contract form from Lynn's book and wrote the list under the words "How Well."

Jeff and his dad agreed to try the new contract the next day.

"What if I miss one day? Does that mean we won't spend special time together on Saturday?" Jeff asked.

"I see what you mean," Joe said. "No one's perfect. Let's say that you will clean your room Monday to Friday and can miss one day a week and still earn the reward. But just one day—no more."

"That sounds fair. I'm going to add a place on the contract where we can check off that I've completed the task each day, so we can keep track."

Jeff made the changes and showed Lynn the new contract.

"It's good you added the days of the week," Lynn said, "so you can check off each time you clean your room. The book calls that a 'task record.' There's one more thing that's missing."

"What's that?" Joe asked.

CONTRACT

TASK

* Who: Jeff

* What: Clean up bedroom

* When: Dad will check room every day after dinner.

* How well:

- Pick up all clothes off floor, bed, desk, and chair.
- Put guitar in case and models and books on shelves.
- Clear top of desk. Put pencils in mug on desk and homework in backpack.
- Make bed.
- Can miss 1 day a week and still get reward.

REWARD

* Who: Dad

* What: Special time with Dad

* When: Saturday

* How much:

3 hours. Jeff's choice: play catch, shoot hoops, ride bikes, go to the batting cage. Jeff can bring a friend if he wants.

M	T	W	Th	F	M	T	W	Th	F	M	T	W	Th	F

Sign here: ___Jeff___ ___Sept 3___

Sign here: ___Dad___ ___Sept 3___

"If you're making Jeff be specific about the task, you have to make the reward specific, too."

"You're right," Joe said. "Jeff, let's fix that before we sign the contract."

Under "Special time with Dad," Joe wrote, "3 hours Jeff's choice: play catch, shoot hoops, ride bikes."

"Put down 'go to the batting cage,' too," Jeff said.

"Okay." Joe added "go to the batting cage" to the contract.

"And can I bring a friend along?" Jeff asked.

His dad nodded and wrote on the contract, "Jeff can bring a friend if he wants."

"I'll check your room each night after dinner," Joe said. He wrote on the contract, "Dad will check room every day after dinner."

"Good," Jeff said, "and I'll look at the list on the contract so I know exactly what I have to do each day."

• • • • •

The next day, Jeff went right to his room when he got home from school. He picked up his contract and looked at the list of things he had to do.

"Hmm, I wonder if that's what it *really* means?" he thought as he read the first part of the task. It said, "Pick up all clothes off floor, bed, desk, and chair."

Jeff did the other tasks on the list. He put his guitar in its case and his models and books on the shelves. He cleared off his desk, put his homework in his backpack, and made his bed.

Then he read the first part again. "Pick up all clothes off floor, bed, desk, and chair."

"Okay, that's what it says, so that's what I'm going to do."

Jeff gathered up his clothes lying around the room. Then he got some clothes from the closet. When he finished, everything looked the way he wanted it to. He closed the door to his room and went outside to play basketball with his friend Perry.

After dinner, he'd find out if contracts *really* worked.

That night, Jeff's parents and sister followed him to his room to see if he had cleaned it up based on what the contract said.

Jeff's sister and mom started to laugh. Then his dad started laughing, too.

"Do I get credit for cleaning up my room, Dad?" Jeff asked.

"You must be kidding!" Joe replied.

"Well, honey, Jeff did do what the contract said," Evelyn reminded Joe. "He picked up all his clothes off the floor, the bed, the chair, and the desk."

One of Jeff's shirts hung over the ceiling fan. Socks hung from the basketball hoop. Underwear was on the doorknob.

"What a loophole!" Joe said.

"What's a loophole?" Jeff asked.

"A loophole is when a contract or rule is written in a way that lets someone do what the words say but not in the way they were meant," Joe said. "You jumped right through a giant loophole in our contract."

Everyone was still smiling at Jeff's joke.

"But you did what our contract says, so I'll give you credit," Joe said. "But let's make the contract more specific, like Lynn suggested."

CONTRACT

TASK

* **Who:** Jeff

* **What:** Clean up bedroom

* **When:** Dad will check room every day after dinner.

* **How well:**

- Pick up all clothes off floor, bed, desk, and chair.
- Put guitar in case and models and books on shelves.
- Clear top of desk. Put pencils in mug on desk and homework in backpack.
- Make bed.
- Can miss 1 day a week and still get reward.

REWARD

* **Who:** Dad

* **What:** Special time with Dad

* **When:** Saturday

* **How much:**

3 hours. Jeff's choice: play catch, shoot hoops, ride bikes, go to the batting cage. Jeff can bring a friend if he wants.

All clothes must be put away in dresser or hung up in closet.   JG JG

M	T	W	Th	F	M	T	W	Th	F	M	T	W	Th	F
X	✓													

Sign here: ___Jeff___   ___Sept 3___

Sign here: ___Dad___   ___Sept 3___

"No problem, Dad. I was just having some fun to see if you and Mom really meant you would follow the contract."

Jeff took a pen and wrote on the contract, "All clothes must be put away in dresser or hung up in closet." Jeff and his dad wrote their initials next to the change to show they both agreed with it.

When Joe checked Jeff's room the next evening, his son had done all the items listed on the contract.

"Everything looks great, Jeff," Joe said.

"Thanks, Dad," Jeff said.

Jeff also decided he would try extra hard to be quiet when he came home from school. That way, his dad would not be tired when he went to work—and when they went to the batting cage on Saturday.

Let's Talk

- What went wrong with Jeff's first contract?
- What was the loophole in Jeff's second contract?
- Why did Jeff use a loophole?
- How did Jeff's family react to his joke?
- How did Jeff and his dad fix the problem in the contract?

3

The Number Problem

Jeff's friend Perry is in fourth grade, too. Perry likes school and wants to do well, but he's having trouble with fractions in math class. Let's see if making a contract with himself can help Perry change that.

"I haven't seen Perry since I got home from work, and he's not outside playing basketball with Jeff," his mom, Keisha, said while getting plates and glasses out for dinner.

"Now that you mention it, I haven't seen him either," his dad, Len, said as he chopped up tomatoes, onions, and cilantro for salsa. "Perry's usually the first one at the table, especially on Taco Tuesday."

Keisha finished setting the table. "He's probably reading and lost track of the time," she said. "I'll go get him."

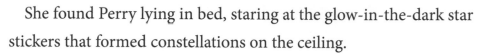

She found Perry lying in bed, staring at the glow-in-the-dark star stickers that formed constellations on the ceiling.

"Everything's ready for tacos, Perry," his mom said.

Usually, Perry would jump up at the mention of food. When he just kept staring at the ceiling, Keisha sat on the bed.

"What's bothering you, Perry? Did something happen at school?"

"I didn't do well on my fractions test," Perry said, covering his face with his arms. "I'm not good at math, and my teacher says you have to be good at math to be a software engineer."

Perry wanted to be a software engineer, like his mom, so he could design video games.

"Well, we all can't be good at everything, but it sounds like you want to do better in math," Keisha said. "Let's eat dinner and talk about it. Figuring out a solution will be easier when we're not so hungry."

During dinner, Perry told his parents he wanted to do better in math, but fractions really confused him.

"I study," Perry said, "but it doesn't do any good."

"Hmm, let's think about what really happens when you say you're going to study," Keisha said. "How often do you play video games instead and then rush through a math worksheet before you stuff it in your backpack to finish in the morning?"

"But I want to have fun, too," Perry said.

"Fair enough," Len said. "We like to relax after work, too. But it sounds like you also want to do better in math. What can you do differently so you can accomplish both?"

"Wait," Keisha said. "I've got an idea that might help. I used to put off writing this weekly report I have to do at work. Then I'd rush to get it done by the end of the day, which was stressful. Plus, my boss thought I could do a better job if I spent more time on it."

"But what does that have to do with my math problem?" Perry asked.

"Your goal is to do a better job on math," Keisha said. "My goal was writing a good report without rushing through it. I figured out a way to do it that might work for you."

"Okay, so what did you do?" Perry asked.

"I decided I would write the report first thing Friday morning and then reward myself with the yoga class I like at lunchtime. Now that I don't rush through the report, it's actually easier to do, and my boss and I are both happier with the result."

"That kind of sounds like what my friend Jeff is doing with his dad," Perry said. "They made a contract to help Jeff keep his room clean. When he keeps it clean all week, Jeff and his dad spend special time together on Saturday."

"Well, Perry," his dad said, "maybe instead of making a contract with me or Mom, you could make a contract with yourself?"

"I don't understand," Perry said. "I thought a contract needed two people."

"You're right. Usually when you make a contract, you agree to do something for another person," Len said. "If you make a contract with yourself, you'd be promising yourself to do a task. Rewarding yourself for doing it will help you to stick to that promise."

His dad had an idea for a contract. "You could agree that you will do math for a half hour before playing any video games on weeknights. That's pretty simple, isn't it?"

"Simple, but not very fun," Perry said.

"Well," Len said, "you're the one who wants to do better at math. To do that, you'll have to put in more time and effort."

"Okay, okay, let's try it," Perry said.

After dinner, Perry and his parents talked more about his contract and printed out a contract form they found online for Perry to fill out.

In the task section, Perry wrote that he would study math for a half hour after dinner Monday through Friday.

In the reward section, he wrote that after he studied math for a half hour, he could play video games for up to an hour until bedtime. To help Perry, his parents agreed to use a timer to keep track of how long he studied.

Perry decided to start on his contract right away. He started a timer and headed back to his bedroom to work on math.

CONTRACT

TASK	REWARD
* Who: Perry	* Who: Perry
* What: Study math	* What: Play video games
* When: Monday to Friday after dinner	* When: When I finish studying
* How well: 1/2 hour	* How much: Up to 1 hour until bedtime

M	T	W	Th	F	M	T	W	Th	F	M	T	W	Th	F

Sign here: _____Perry_____ Oct 28

Sign here: _____Perry_____ Oct 28

For two weeks straight, Perry studied for a half hour Monday through Friday, looking over the math lesson in his textbook. Perry followed his contract. But it didn't help. Fractions still confused him, and he didn't do any better on the next math test.

"Maybe I'm not smart enough to do better in math," he told his parents at dinner.

"I think it's more likely that we need to take a look at the contract and think about why it's not working," his mom said. "We all thought your grade would improve if you spent more time studying. But your goal isn't really about time. It's about *doing* better in math. Why don't you try a new contract with a different approach?"

"Like what?" Perry asked.

"We can get some fraction problems, like the ones that are giving

you trouble, off the website your teacher recommended," Len said. "Each weeknight after dinner, you can work on solving ten problems. That will be the task you promise to do."

He also pointed out the task could take more or less than a half hour.

"Once you solve all ten problems correctly, you can play video games," Len said.

"If you have trouble, you can ask one of us for help," Keisha said.

Perry agreed to try this and rewrote his contract to say that he'd solve ten fraction problems each night. When he had told his friend Jeff about the contract he'd made with himself, Jeff showed Perry the official seal he'd drawn for his family's contracts. Jeff explained that the official seal helps show that a contract is serious. Perry liked this idea. He added a basketball sticker to the bottom of his new contract for his own official seal.

Jeff also told Perry that he liked seeing how well he was doing with his contract, so his sister helped him create a "task record"—an easy way to track his progress. Jeff told Perry he had agreed to clean up his room each day Monday through Friday so he marked off each day on his contract and marked off each day after he cleaned his room.

Perry decided to create his own task record. He had to study only Monday through Friday so he listed just those days in one row and put a blank row underneath to it. Each day he did what he promised to do in the contract, he planned to put a check mark under that day.

CONTRACT

TASK

* Who: Perry

* What: ~~Study math~~
  Solve fraction problems

* When: Monday to Friday
  after dinner

* How well: ~~1/2 hour~~

  Solve 10 problems like
  the ones that give me
  trouble at school. Mom
  or Dad will check my
  work and explain extra
  hard ones.

REWARD

* Who: Perry

* What: Play video games

* When: When I finish
  studying

* How much:

  Up to 1 hour until bedtime

M	T	W	Th	F	M	T	W	Th	F	M	T	W	Th	F
✓	✓	✓	✓	✓	✓	✓	✓	✓	✓	✓	✓	✓	✓	✓

Sign here: ___Perry___ ___Oct 28___

Sign here: ___Perry___ ___Oct 28___

Now Perry knew exactly what he had to do each weeknight—solve ten problems and ask his parents for help if he needed it—and as soon as he got them done, he could play video games. That was better than before, when he spent a lot of time looking at the clock just waiting for the half hour to be over.

Perry worked hard on the problems. Each day, he felt like he understood fractions better.

When Perry got his report card three weeks later, his math grade had gone up. His teacher added a comment about how impressed she was that he had worked so hard to understand fractions. In fact, she said she planned to show all the kids in her class how they could make their own contracts.

Let's Talk

- Why didn't Perry's first contract work?
- How did Perry and his parents fix the problem?
- How do you think Perry felt when he got his report card?
- Do you think you might want to make a contract with yourself?

4

The Pet Menace

Maya, a four-year-old with autism, plays too rough with the family pets. Jeff told Maya's sister, Martina, about his contract with his dad to clean up his room, and Perry told her about his self-contract to do better in math. Martina wonders if a contract could help little Maya.

Maya stacked a bunch of her building blocks and climbed on them to reach the fish tank on the shelf in the living room. She dropped smaller blocks into the tank because she liked to see the fish swim fast.

Maya was getting ready to drop another block into the tank when her mom, Camila, entered the room.

"Stop that, Maya!"

The little girl whirled around and dropped the block on the floor. Her older sister, Martina, heard the noise from the kitchen and came to help. Martina lifted her sister down from the stack of blocks.

"Poor fish," Martina said as she pulled some blocks out of the tank. Martina then went back to the kitchen to get the popcorn she had been making. She pulled the popcorn bag out of the microwave, put it in a bowl to cool, and then carried it into the living room.

Maya headed for the popcorn while her dad, Roberto, unstacked the large blocks Maya had climbed on. He put them on a shelf Maya couldn't reach.

"I wish we could do something about the way she treats the pets, especially the dog," Camila said.

"Me, too," Martina said. "Maya, if you're not trying to hurt the goldfish, you're pulling Bella's tail or pinching her ears."

Maya ignored them. She kept eating popcorn.

"Well, one way to end this problem is to find a new home for the dog and those fish," Roberto said.

"Daddy, no!" Martina said.

"Roberto, I don't think that's a good solution," Camila said. "Martina loves Bella, and it's important for Maya to learn how to be kind to animals."

"I agree, but we constantly scold her about the pets, and it doesn't do any good," Roberto said.

"I've got an idea!" Martina said.

Everyone stopped talking and looked at her. Even Maya stopped reaching for more popcorn.

"My friends Jeff and Perry told me about something called 'contracts' their families are using to help solve problems," Martina said. "A contract lists a task that somebody is supposed to do and a reward they'll get for doing it. Let's make a contract with Maya for being nice to Bella and the fish."

"Contack!" Maya yelled between mouthfuls of popcorn.

"Maya's only four and doesn't read," Roberto said. "She won't know what a contract says."

"Does a contract have to be written in words?" Martina said.

"How else would you do it?" Camila asked.

"We can use pictures," Martina said. "We'll cut out pictures and make drawings to show the things in Maya's contract that we want her to do. Then we'll explain it to her and tape it next to the fish tank to remind her. And since the fish are near Bella's dog bed, hopefully that will remind her to be kind to Bella, too."

"That's a good idea, Martina," Camila said.

"Let's give it a try," Roberto said.

Camila grabbed a stack of old magazines and said, "We should be able to find pictures in these."

Martina and her parents started looking through the magazines, while Maya kept eating popcorn. Before long, they found a photo of a girl playing happily with a dog.

"This one's good," Martina said.

Martina went to her room and came back with a piece of paper, scissors, tape, and markers. She drew a line in the middle from top to bottom, cut out the photo, and taped it to the left side of the paper.

"Let's add some happy fish," Martina said.

She drew a picture of a girl looking at a bowl with two goldfish inside.

"That looks great," her dad said. "Those pictures will remind Maya to play nicely with Bella and watch the fish swim instead of bothering them. That will be the task part of her contract."

"Now, what are we going to put on the right side of the contract to show Maya's reward for doing her task?" Camila asked.

They didn't wonder for long. Maya came over to the stack of magazines. She picked up one and held it out to her sister.

"Book," she said.

Everyone laughed. They could all see what the reward should be. One of Maya's favorite things was to have someone read to her. Camila arranged three of her daughter's favorite books on the coffee table, took a photo of them with her phone, and printed out the picture.

Martina taped the photo of the books to the right side of the paper.

"There's one more thing we need," Martina said as she started sketching a picture of her favorite animal. "Jeff and Perry said creating your family's own official seal and putting it on a contract shows that the contract is important. I'm going to draw a butterfly. Maya loves them."

Martina drew a butterfly with a blue background for the sky. "Here's your contract, Maya," she said, holding out the paper.

Her little sister grabbed the paper and smiled. Then Camila took her hand, pointed to the pictures, and explained what each one meant.

CONTRACT

TASK

REWARD

Mom   Dad

Martina

"See how the girl is playing nicely with her dog?" she said. "Come here, Bella. See, Maya, how I'm petting Bella gently? No hitting. And I'm not touching her ears or tail. You try it now."

Maya petted Bella's back just like her mom had.

Then Martina pointed to the drawing of the girl with the two smiling fish. She walked Maya over to the fish tank and talked to her sister about watching the fish swim. She held her hands gently and said, "Remember, Maya, just look—no hands or toys in the water."

Maya got most excited when her dad pointed to the photo of the books. Roberto explained how someone would read her an extra story before she went to bed. To get the reward, she had to be good to the pets from the time she got home from preschool in the afternoon until bedtime.

"Okay, Papa," Maya said.

To be sure Maya really understood what was expected, Martina demonstrated each task again and then practiced each one with her little sister.

Martina and her parents signed the bottom of the contract. Martina handed a marker to her little sister and asked her to color on the bottom. Maya scribbled on the paper.

"There, Maya, now you have our family's first official contract," Martina said, taking the marker back and giving Maya a high five.

"Contack! Contack!" Maya said, and she jumped up and down happily.

Then Martina showed Maya she was taping the contract to the fish tank to remind her to be nice to the pets.

• • • • •

The next afternoon when Maya came home from preschool, she went right to the fish tank. Her mother held her breath as Maya reached out for the fish, but her younger daughter just pointed to the paper hanging there and said, "Contack!"

Maya played with her building blocks until dinner was ready, and she didn't go near the fish again. Camila sighed with relief. Her daughter seemed to remember her contract and understand what the pictures meant.

After dinner, Maya sat near the fish tank and stared at the shiny fish darting around in the water. She kept her hands in her lap. She looked over to see what her family would do because she was sitting so close to the fish.

Everyone seemed to be ignoring her, so Maya moved closer to the tank. But no one paid any attention to her like they usually did. Maya stood and moved closer to the fish. Still nothing.

She stacked up some books so she could be eye level with the fish tank—so close her nose almost touched the glass. Everyone acted like she wasn't even there. She waited a little longer. Then she splashed one of her hands into the water.

"Maya, no!" everyone said and rushed over to move her away from the fish.

"I knew it was too good to be true," Camila said. "Just when I thought it might really work."

"Me, too," Roberto said. "Maya is just too young to understand a contract."

"No, wait," Martina said. "I think Maya does understand her contract. It's the rest of us who don't."

"What do you mean?" Roberto asked.

"Well, a contract says if you do something, then something good will happen. You'll get a reward. That makes you want to do that task again. Right?"

Her parents nodded.

"Okay, Maya did what she was supposed to do. She played nicely and didn't bother the fish or hurt Bella for two hours, but nothing good happened. We just ignored her."

"But nothing was *supposed* to happen," Roberto said. "Maya's contract said she couldn't bother the pets all evening. *Then* she would get her story."

"That's just what I mean," Martina said. "We made a contract that asked too much of a little kid like Maya."

"I think I see what you're trying to tell us," Camila said. "The whole evening must seem like years to Maya. She was being perfectly good, but we all ignored her."

"And the only way she could get our attention was to reach into the water," Martina said. "I think our contract with Maya will work if she gets a reward for shorter bits of time."

"But we can't read her a story every five or ten minutes," Roberto said.

Martina agreed. "Let's change Maya's contract so she gets one story before dinner and another one before she goes to bed. Then she has to be good to Bella and the fish for less time before she gets a reward."

"But even an hour might be too long for Maya," her mom said.

"I know. But we can pay attention to her when we see her trying," Martina said. "She kept creeping closer and closer to the fish tank and watching us all the time. But we didn't say anything. Finally, she couldn't stand it anymore."

"You might be right," Roberto agreed. "If she'll act up to get our attention, she just might behave to get it, too. It's worth a try."

"Okay," Martina said. "From now on when any of us sees that

Maya is playing and not bugging the fish, we'll tell her how proud we are of her for being kind to the animals. And that goes for when she's playing nicely with Bella, too."

"With all of us helping, I know she can do it," Camila said.

The next night, Maya accomplished her contract. And nearly every night after that.

Let's Talk

- What did Maya do to hurt the dog and the fish?
- What could she do to be kind to them?
- Since Maya couldn't read, how did her family make a contract she could understand?
- How do you think Martina felt for suggesting a picture contract for her little sister?

5

Lynn Pitches In

Evelyn and Joe had been unhappy that their kids weren't doing their chores. Jeff made a contract with his dad to clean up his room. Now Jeff's sister, Lynn, makes a contract with their mom to start dinner when she gets home from school.

When Evelyn walked through the front door, she heard her daughter, Lynn, talking on the phone. Lynn was supposed to get dinner started before her mom got home, but Evelyn didn't smell anything cooking.

Lynn quickly said goodbye when she saw her mom.

"Lynn, you know I need your help."

"I'm sorry I didn't get dinner started, Mom," Lynn said. "I lost track of the time."

"That happens a lot," Evelyn said. "Something has to change, and I have an idea. Jeff's done really well with his room-cleaning contract. Maybe a contract would help you, too."

Lynn smiled and said, "You're right! I'll go write one up, like Jeff's."

She hurried to her room. Ten minutes later, Lynn handed her mom a contract form. She'd filled in the task, and Jeff had drawn their family's official seal—an image of their house—at the bottom.

After Evelyn read it, Lynn asked, "How does it sound? Should we sign it and make it official?"

"Well, Lynn, you've done well being specific about the task— start dinner by 4:30 p.m. Monday through Friday, following the instructions that Dad or I leave for you—but the reward side is empty."

"I don't mind starting dinner, Mom," Lynn said. "It doesn't take that long, and I like cooking. Also, I know you're tired after work, and helping out makes me feel good. I don't need a reward."

"That's sweet of you, but Jeff is getting special time with Dad for cleaning up his room. You should get a reward, too. I know you like craft projects and that you've been wanting to get a new desk for your room. How about this? Starting tomorrow, if you do what the contract says for three weeks without missing more than one day, you and I will go to the flea market at the end of the month and buy a desk for you to refinish."

"That would be awesome!" Lynn said.

Evelyn filled in the reward part of the contract. Lynn and her mom signed it. Then they put it on the refrigerator door, where her parents

CONTRACT

TASK

* **Who:** Lynn

* **What:** Help prepare dinner using instructions left by Mom or Dad

* **When:** Monday–Friday start by 4:30 p.m.

* **How well:**

   Monday–Friday for 3 weeks (can miss 1 day)

REWARD

* **Who:** Mom

* **What:** Go to flea market with Mom to buy a desk

* **When:** End of the month

* **How much:**

   Reasonably priced desk

M	T	W	Th	F	M	T	W	Th	F	M	T	W	Th	F
✓	✓	✓	✓											

Sign here: _Lynn_ _Sept 10_

Sign here: _Mom_ _Sept 10_

left the dinner instructions, to remind them what they had both agreed to do.

Lynn arrived home at 4:00 p.m. the next day. When the alarm she'd set on her phone went off a half hour later, she headed for the kitchen. By 5:00 p.m., she had chicken and potatoes baking in the oven. She was cutting tomatoes and cucumbers for a salad when her mom came home.

"Lynn, how nice! It looks like dinner's almost ready."

"Thanks, Mom. How was your day?"

"Good, thanks. Now, why don't you get a head start on your homework. I'll finish making the salad and set the table. You can wake up your dad now, too. I'll call everyone when dinner's ready."

After dinner, Lynn went online to look for instructions on how to refinish a secondhand desk. She found lots of good ideas and was excited about cooking dinner the next few weeks so she could get started on her own desk project.

Let's Talk

- What chores are you supposed to do?
- Do you sometimes forget to do your chores?
- Would a contract help you remember to do your chores?
- Where would you hang a contract as a reminder?

6

By Myself

Connor, a fourth-grader with autism, is in the same class as Jeff, Perry, and Martina. Connor has trouble getting ready for school, which makes mornings hectic and stressful for him and his mom. Will a contract help get their days off to a better start?

Krista, a behavior analyst who helps kids with their behavior, was visiting Connor at home to see how he was doing. While Krista and Connor's mom, Eriko, talked, Connor was busy building a tower out of Lego blocks.

"Krista, Connor is doing great with his schoolwork," Eriko said, "but we're having trouble in the morning getting him ready to catch the school bus on time. We've gone over what he's supposed to do to get ready on his own, but it isn't working. Then I step in to hurry him along, things get unpleasant, and we both end up having a bad start to the day. Any ideas?"

"There are several things we can try," Krista said. "One is to use something called a 'behavior contract' to help Connor get ready in the morning."

"Interesting that you mention a contract," Eriko said. "My friend Camila told me she's using one with her daughter Maya, who also has autism. The contract is helping her learn to play nicely with their pets. Camila said the contract uses pictures because Maya is too young to read. I don't think Connor would need to have pictures because he reads so well."

Krista took a file folder from her bag. "Because contracts work for many families, I carry examples of different contract forms with me."

Krista explained to Eriko that all contracts have two main parts: a task and a reward. The first step in making a contract is to select the task.

"So what exactly would you like to see Connor do by himself to get ready for school?" Krista asked.

"I'd like him to get dressed, make his bed, eat breakfast and put his dirty dishes in the sink, wash his face and brush his teeth, check that his homework is in his backpack, and be at the door watching for the bus at seven forty-five. I know that's a lot. I don't expect him to do this all right away."

"Well, how about we start with these four steps?" Krista said.

She wrote them down on the contract.

TASK: GET READY FOR SCHOOL

- Get dressed (lay out clothes and shoes the night before).

- Eat breakfast and put dirty dishes in the sink.

- Wash face and brush teeth.

- Be at front door with backpack (get it ready the night before) at 7:45 a.m.

"Even though Connor can read," she said, "we can make his contract more personal by using words and photos of Connor doing each step, so he can quickly see what he's supposed to do next."

"Sounds good," Eriko said. "But what about the reward?"

"Almost every time I come over, Connor is building with Lego pieces," Krista said. "Maybe Connor could earn new pieces for doing the task on his contract. Do you think that would work as a reward?"

"I do," Eriko said. "Connor keeps talking about a set of ten small Lego characters he wants. It's inexpensive and something I'd probably get for him anyway. Let's talk to Connor and see what he thinks about our contract idea."

Krista and Eriko explained to Connor how a contract might help him get ready in the morning. He liked the idea, and with help from his mom and Krista, he filled in the contract before Krista left.

The next day was Saturday, so Eriko and Connor had plenty of time to take and print out photos of Connor doing each of the four steps on the Get Ready for School list. They glued the four photos to the contract.

Then Eriko attached Velcro to four Lego blocks and a strip of Velcro next to each photo. As Connor finished each step of the task, he would attach a block next to it. This would help him track how close he was to being ready to go.

Eriko had also printed out a little picture of Lego pieces. She told Connor she did this to make their family's own official seal, which shows the contract is important.

To create a task record to track Connor's progress, they also drew a row of boxes on the contract to represent Monday to Friday. Eriko showed Connor a roll of Lego stickers. Each morning Connor did what the contract said, he could put one of the stickers on that day of the week. After school that same day, she would give him a new Lego character. Connor also had the chance to earn a bonus reward. If he completed the tasks all five school days in a week, he'd get an extra Lego character.

Finally, they each signed the contract.

After a few weeks with his contract, Connor was doing well. It took him a week or two to get the hang of it, but he and his mom didn't give up. Once he started getting himself ready in the mornings, Connor felt proud. He really liked earning a bonus character for making his contract all five days in a week. He was also happy his mom was proud of him. Connor even started to make his bed in the morning when he had time, and he often did now that getting ready was so much easier.

CONTRACT

TASK

* **Who:** Connor

* **What:** Get ready for school by 7:45 a.m.

* **When:** Each school day

* **How well:**

  Complete entire task for daily reward. Perfect week earns bonus reward!

REWARD

* **Who:** Mom

* **What:** Lego characters

* **When:** After school each day task is completed. Bonus reward on Friday.

* **How much:**

  1 character per day. 1 extra character for perfect week.

BONUS! →

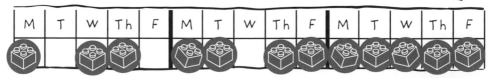

| M | T | W | Th | F | M | T | W | Th | F | M | T | W | Th | F |

Sign here: Connor   Nov 6

Sign here: Mom   Nov 6

Let's Talk

- What are mornings like at your house?
- What were mornings like for Connor and his mom before their contract?
- Do you think the photos on Connor's contract helped him?
- How did Connor feel when he got himself ready on time?

7

Siblings United

Contracts were a success for Jeff, who's cleaning up his room without reminders, and Lynn, who's starting dinner for the family. Now this brother and sister decide to make a contract with each other.

As he came into the house after school, Jeff heard music playing and his sister singing. Lynn stopped and looked up as her brother entered the kitchen.

"What's for dinner?" Jeff asked.

"Spaghetti, green beans, and a salad," Lynn said.

Lynn's task was to help prepare dinner, and she had been trying hard to get this chore done right after school.

"I love spaghetti. Can I help you make dinner so I can learn how to make it? Maybe you could teach me how to cook some other things, too."

"Thanks, but it would take a lot longer if I had to show you how to do everything. I want to get dinner going as fast as I can so I can work on a big project for my room."

"You never spend any time with me anymore," Jeff said. "And what big project are you talking about, anyway?"

"Thanks to my contract with Mom, I got a desk at the flea market. I'm starting to refinish it now. I have to sand it before I can paint it, and sanding takes a long time."

"Okay, I get it," Jeff said. "Hey, I've got an idea."

"By the look in your eye, I can tell you're up to something, little brother."

"Well, kids can have contracts with each other, right? Why don't *we* work one out?"

"I had a feeling you were thinking about something like that," Lynn said. "Well, why not? How about if I give you a cooking lesson while I'm making dinner, then you help me sand or paint my desk that night for half an hour? That would be a fair trade, wouldn't it?"

"Would you explain all the recipe steps and let me try to do everything?"

"Sure, but this contract would be only for a few weeks until we get my desk done. By then, though, you'll know enough to do some cooking on your own."

"Then it's a deal," Jeff said. "I've got to clean up my room now. After dinner, let's figure out the details and make our own contract."

CONTRACT

TASK

* **Who:** Lynn

* **What:** Cooking lessons for Jeff

* **When:** When Lynn is starting dinner (if she can/wants to)

* **How well:**

    Lynn will explain each recipe step and let Jeff try to do everything

REWARD

* **Who:** Jeff

* **What:** Help Lynn refinish her desk

* **When:** After dinner each night that Jeff gets a cooking lesson

* **How much:**

    Jeff will help sand or paint Lynn's desk for 30 minutes

M	T	W	Th	F	M	T	W	Th	F	M	T	W	Th	F
✓	✓	✓												

Sign here: _Lynn_ _____ Nov 13 _____

Sign here: _Jeff_ _____ Nov 13 _____

Note: This contract will be in effect for 3 weeks

Over the next few weeks, Lynn taught Jeff how to make some of his favorite dishes, including spaghetti, roast chicken, and mac and cheese. He was so excited about cooking, he decided to make a whole meal for the family on the weekend.

Lynn's refinished desk looked beautiful, too. Next, she planned to pick out some fabric and have her mom show her how to sew new curtains for her room.

Jeff and Lynn were both happy with the results of their contract. Jeff learned to cook, and Lynn got her desk done faster. They also got along better after spending more time together. That was an extra bonus.

Let's Talk

- How did the contract benefit both Lynn and Jeff?

- Would you want to make a contract with your sister or brother, if you have one?

- If you made a contract with a sibling, what would the task and the reward be?

- Would you want your parents to help you make a contract? If so, how could they help?

8

Now It's Your Turn, Mom and Dad

Jeff and Lynn are doing their contract tasks, and the family is getting along much better. But their parents keep reminding them to do their chores, making Jeff and Lynn feel like they're being nagged. The kids propose a contract for their parents. This should be interesting.

Evelyn arrived home to find her son shooting hoops in the driveway.

"Hi, Jeff. How was school today?"

"Fine."

"Don't forget to clean up your room."

"Mom, you know I'll do it. I've hardly missed a day in the last month. Why do you have to keep bugging me about it?"

"Sorry. I guess it's just a habit."

Fifteen minutes later, Jeff's dad called out from his bedroom, "Lynn, are you getting dinner started? You know I can't be late for work."

"Yes, Dad," Lynn said. "I'm working on it right now."

Since the family had started using contracts, they talked once a week after dinner about how things were going and their plans for the week.

At the meeting that night, Evelyn spoke first.

"A month ago, I never would have thought things would be going so well. Jeff, your room is almost always neat, and you've been much quieter in the afternoon when your dad's sleeping."

Joe smiled and winked at his son.

"Lynn, it's so nice to come home and have dinner nearly ready," Evelyn said. "Best of all, we're all getting along a lot better."

Lynn spoke up. "Maybe our problem was that we all complained about each other, instead of trying to figure out what was wrong and how to fix it."

"That makes sense," her dad said while Evelyn nodded in agreement.

"Something is bugging Jeff and me though," Lynn said.

"What?" Joe asked.

"Dad, as soon as you wake up, you ask me if I've got dinner ready."

Jeff added, "Mom, as soon as you get home from work, you ask me if I've cleaned up my room. We want you to stop nagging us so much. You just said you know we're doing what we're supposed to."

"We're sorry," Joe said. "I guess nagging is just a habit."

"Well, Jeff and I have an idea," Lynn said. "We want you two to sign a contract."

"You want to have a contract with us?" Joe asked.

"Yes. If you want to be fair, you should be willing to make some changes, too," Lynn said.

"Joe, they've got a point," Evelyn said. "Maybe we're just used to nagging them to do things because we always had to remind them before."

"So, it's okay if Jeff and I draw up a contract for you?" Lynn asked.

"We can try it," Evelyn said.

"I'll get a blank contract from my room."

When Lynn came back with a form, she said, "My teacher said a contract task should describe what you will do, not what you shouldn't do. We want you to stop nagging us. What can you do instead?"

"How about we don't ask when you're going to do your tasks?" Evelyn said. "But after you're done, we can say thank you."

"That sounds good," Lynn said. "We'll give you a check mark every day you don't nag and just thank us when we're done."

"If you can go five weekdays in a row without reminding us to do our tasks, you'll earn a reward," Jeff said. "But if you remind us, we start over counting the five days."

"What's our reward?" Joe asked.

"Jeff and I will make a special dinner the next weekend and do all the cleanup," Lynn said.

"Works for me," Joe said.

"Let's do it," Evelyn said.

The family filled out the rest of the contract, Jeff drew their family's official seal on it, and everyone signed it.

"I'll put the contract on the refrigerator so we can all see how it's going," Jeff said.

• • • • •

Two weeks later, Jeff and Lynn were peeling and slicing vegetables for a special weekend dinner for their mom and dad. The first week, their parents had slipped and reminded them about doing their chores. Now, five weekdays had gone by without their parents asking them when they were going to do their tasks. When their mom came

CONTRACT

TASK	REWARD
* Who: Mom and Dad	*** Who:** Lynn and Jeff
* What: Thank Lynn and Jeff for doing their contract tasks instead of nagging them	*** What:** Special dinner for Mom and Dad
* When: Every day	*** When:** Weekend night picked by Mom and Dad
* How well: No nags for 5 days in a row	*** How much:** Lynn and Jeff will make Mom and Dad's favorite dishes and clean up

M	T	W	Th	F	M	T	W	Th	F	M	T	W	Th	F
✓	✗	✓	✓	✗	✓	✓	✓	✓	✓					

Sign here: _Lynn   Jeff_   _Nov 22_

Sign here: _Dad   Mom_   _Nov 22_

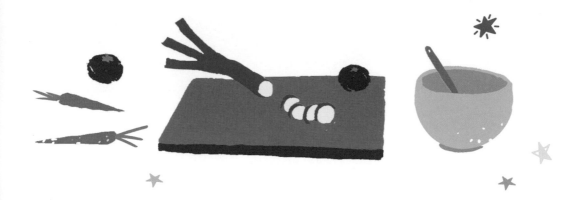

home from work, she'd say something nice about the dinner Lynn was preparing, and their dad made it a point to admire Jeff's clean room on a regular basis.

Everyone agreed that making contracts really helped the family get along better. And they had fun doing it!

Let's Talk

- How is this contract different from those in the other stories?

- The kids' goal was to stop their parents from nagging them to do their chores. How did the family make the parents' task a positive action?

- If you could have your parent sign a contract, what would the task and the reward be?

9

Making Friends

Connor is sad because he feels like he doesn't have any friends. Connor's mom, Eriko; his teacher, Janelle Gardner; and Krista, a behavior analyst who helps Connor learn new skills, want to help him make friends. Let's see how a contract that rewards Connor for talking to kids works out.

Eriko and Krista waited in Janelle Gardner's classroom until she had finished getting all her students onto buses for the ride home. When the teacher returned, she joined Eriko and Krista at a table near the back of the room.

"Thank you for meeting with us, Ms. Gardner," Eriko said.

"Please call me Janelle," Connor's teacher said. "Let me start by saying that Connor has been doing very well with his schoolwork."

"That's great to hear," Eriko said. "The problem is that Connor has been coming home upset because he says he doesn't have any friends at school."

"I understand how Connor could feel left out," Janelle said. "Most of my students have known each other since kindergarten. Since Connor is new this year, the other kids don't know much about him. When I have the class work in small groups, Connor tends to hang back. Do you have ideas about how to help him make friends?"

"Krista and I made this contract to help Connor get ready for school by himself," Eriko said, handing the contract to Janelle. "Connor's been doing great with it for several weeks now. In fact, we're about to end the contract because Connor says he can get ready by himself and doesn't need it anymore. Maybe we could work out a contract to help Connor make friends."

Janelle looked over the contract. "I've made contracts with students for tasks like doing their homework. Recently, one of my students who wanted to get better at math made his own contract. I'll bet we could come up with a contract that would help Connor make friends."

"We should start simply," Krista said. "Making friends can be hard. A contract that rewards Connor for talking to a classmate might be a good first step."

"I like that idea," Eriko said.

"Me, too," Janelle agreed. "Let's call the task: 'Talk to another student.'"

The three women discussed what Connor would need to do to

complete the task of talking to another student. Janelle wrote down their ideas.

- Check that the student you want to talk to isn't busy or talking with somebody else.

- Say "Hi" and greet the person by name.

- Ask a question about something the other person might like: "Do you play baseball?" or "Have you been to the new park?"

- Listen to the answer and don't interrupt.

- Respond to the student's answer politely: "That's interesting" or "That's cool." Or ask another question: "What's your favorite baseball team?" or "Have you tried the new climbing wall?"

- Tell them something about yourself: "I played baseball over the summer" or "The new climbing wall is hard."

"Wow. That sounds like a lot for anyone, and Connor is shy," Eriko said.

"To make it easier, we can write out simpler steps that Connor can practice with you at home," Krista said. "When he feels comfortable, he can try talking to kids at school."

Janelle wrote these steps for Connor:

HOW TO TALK TO ANOTHER STUDENT

- Greet student by name and say "Hi."

- Ask a question.

- Listen to the answer. Don't interrupt.

- Reply to the student's answer or ask another question.

- Say something about yourself.

"With your permission, Eriko, I'll talk with a few students who are very kind," Janelle said. "I'll tell them Connor wants to make friends and ask them to talk with him, so he can practice."

"That would be great," Eriko said. "Thank you."

"I'll pair Connor with these same students during class, so they can get to know each other better," the teacher added. "To begin, I suggest Connor's contract says he should talk to another student once or twice a day. He can do this at lunch or during recess. He can also do this in the classroom during free time or when small groups are working together."

"Could you let me know how it goes?" Eriko asked.

"Before he heads for the bus home, Connor can tell me what happened that day," Janelle said. "I'll praise all efforts, even if he doesn't think they went well. I'll send a note home each day saying if he talked to kids and how it went."

"But how about the reward?" Krista asked. "A contract needs a reward."

"I'll talk with Connor tonight about our contract idea," Eriko said. "If he wants to try it, I'll ask what he would like for the reward, and then we'll finish the contract form together."

"Sounds great," Janelle said.

The three women said goodbye, and Eriko and Krista headed home.

• • • • •

That night, Eriko showed her son the contract and the list and explained how the first step to making friends was talking to other kids. Connor was proud of how well the contract for getting ready for school had gone and liked the idea of making a contract for the task "talk to another student." He felt that was a task he could do, and practicing would make it easier.

For the reward, Connor and his mom decided that each day he completed the task, he could choose one of three things: watch a favorite science video, plant a seedling for the garden, or have a special after-school snack. He would also place a check mark on a task record listing school days to show his progress.

After filling out the new contract, Connor and his mom signed it. Then they added a picture of Lego characters—the same one they had used for Connor's Get Ready for School contract—as their family's official seal.

The next day, Connor told his teacher he wanted to try the contract. Ms. Gardner gave him the list of steps she had written out

CONTRACT

TASK

* **Who:** Connor

* **What:** Talk to another student

* **When:** Each day at school during lunch, recess, free time, or group activities

* **How well:**

- Practice for 3–5 minutes with students selected by teacher
- Start conversation with another student
- Tell Ms. Gardner how talks went
- Take Ms. Gardner's note home and tell Mom about the talks

REWARD

* **Who:** Mom

* **What:**

Connor's choice:
- Watch a favorite science video
- Plant a seedling for the garden
- Have a special after-school snack

* **When:** After school

* **How much:**

1 reward each day he talks to another student

M	T	W	Th	F	M	T	W	Th	F	M	T	W	Th	F
✓	✓	✓	✓	✗	✓	✗	✓	✓	✓	✓				

Sign here: Connor   Feb 14

Sign here: Mom Janelle Gardner   Feb 14

for how to talk to another student. She explained how he could use it to practice.

For the next few days, Connor's mom and Krista took turns practicing the steps with him. Then Ms. Gardner helped Connor practice with a few kids in his class for short periods of time.

Next, Connor practiced starting a conversation on his own. That was scary, and he skipped a couple of days. But his teacher and mom encouraged him to try again, and it got easier.

Connor brought the notes home from his teacher and proudly showed them to his mom. Each day he tried to talk to another kid, Connor put a check mark on the task record of his contract and chose his reward.

It helped that the kids who had practiced with him also would come over and talk to him, too. After a couple of weeks, Connor realized that he was talking to another student every day, and on some days he talked to more than one student.

"Ms. Gardner says I'm doing great, Mom," Connor said one day after school. "Jeff, Perry, and Martina talk with me all the time now, and sometimes we play catch at recess."

Several weeks later, Connor hopped off the school bus with a huge grin on his face.

"Connor, what's up? You look so excited," his mom said.

"My friend Perry invited me to his birthday party! His mom will send you the information. Perry likes playing baseball like I do, so maybe I could get him a new baseball cap for a birthday present. Can I go?"

"Of course. You'll have a great time," his mom said while hugging him and blinking back happy tears.

Let's Talk

- Connor wanted to make friends at school. How did his contract help him?
- How did the list of steps help Connor?
- How did practicing with other kids help Connor?
- If you had a contract with your teacher, what task and what reward would you choose?

PART II

Make
Your Own
Contracts

**Select
the task**

**Choose the
reward**

**Write the
contract**

**Implement
the contract**

Contracting is a positive way to change your child's behavior.

IN THIS CHAPTER, YOU'LL LEARN:

- What a contract is

- The parts of a contract

- How contracts can help resolve behavior problems

- How contracts can help achieve personal goals

10

What Is Contracting?

No matter how caring and energetic you are, you're not alone if you're a parent who often struggles with the demands placed upon you every day. Juggling work, childcare, household tasks, school, and other responsibilities—not to mention trying to carve out a little time for yourself or with your partner—is challenging enough on a good day. It's no wonder disagreements arise with children about chores, homework, and other routine tasks, causing tension and conflict for all family members.

In an ideal world, you'd turn to simple solutions, guaranteed to solve all problems. But, of course, there is no easy or magical fix. Life is too complicated for that. Parents—indeed anyone, from teachers to grandparents, who works with kids—need a range of tools to deal with a variety of situations. Behavior contracting, the strategy described in this book, is a tool you can use to resolve behavior problems in a positive manner. Contracting can also help any family member, including you, achieve personal goals.

We define *contracting* as a teaching strategy that asks a child to do a specific task and promises a reward that follows successful completion of that task. Dozens of research studies have demonstrated the effectiveness of contracting for improving behavior and teaching new skills to children of all ages, with and without special needs, in home, school, and community settings (see References).

Benefits of Family Contracts

Contracting offers a positive approach to address more challenging behaviors, including:

- Fighting with siblings
- Not following directions
- Arguing
- Throwing tantrums
- Refusing to do chores
- Not doing homework

But the benefits of contracts go beyond resolving behavior problems. Contracts can also motivate your child to:

- Become more independent in many areas of daily living
- Achieve personal goals such as learning to play an instrument or exercising regularly

- Develop new interests or hobbies

- Learn new skills ranging from talking to other kids (see the story "Making Friends") to cooking (see the story "Siblings United")

You can also create contracts with your partner or yourself to change the way you interact with your child or each another. For example, a contract might be helpful if you want to:

- Pay more attention to your child's appropriate behavior

- Spend more one-on-one time with your child

- Spend more time with your partner

Here's what makes the contracts described in this book different from typical verbal agreements parents often make with their kids:

- The agreement is put in writing.

- The language describing the task and the reward is very specific and clearly understood by everyone.

- The child's and parent's signatures (or a personal mark from a child who does not write) indicate each individual's commitment to give the contract an honest try.

- When displayed, the written contract serves as a visual reminder to the child and parent about what they've each agreed to do.

Parts of a Contract

The main parts of a behavior contract are:

- **Task:** a promised action (usually something your child will do)

- **Reward:** a promised positive consequence (typically provided by you)

- **Signatures:** signed names or a personal mark (for a child who doesn't write) of the people making the contract

- **Official seal:** a small image that personalizes the contract for your family and signifies its importance

- **Task record:** visual way to track each time the task is completed successfully

As an example, we'll look at a contract for a common problem faced by parents—getting young children to go to bed peacefully and on time—to illustrate these contract elements. Six-year-old Lily's usual evening routine included playing with her puzzles and collection of small ceramic animals, arguing about going to bed, pleading to stay up longer, crying, asking for a drink or snack, and sometimes erupting into a full-blown tantrum when her parents didn't consent. Lily's unwillingness to go to bed and the many ways she resisted her parents created much stress and made most nights unpleasant.

Lily's parents created the contract shown on the following page to help their daughter learn to go to bed at her bedtime and stay there through the night. In addition to the contract, Lily's parents made sure she had dinner and her bath early enough to allow time for playing, a few stories with mom or dad, and a light snack and drink before bedtime.

How a Contract Describes the Task

To describe the task—what your child promises to do—on a contract form, you fill in four pieces of information *Who, What, When,* and *How Well.* You can copy the contract forms in this book or download and print forms from contractingwithkids.com. We'll use Lily's bedtime contract to give an example of each:

- **Who:** The person who will perform the task and receive the reward—in this case, Lily.

- **What:** The behavior or task the person must do to earn the reward—Lily will go to bed.

- **When:** The time the task must be completed. Lily needs go to bed at 8:30 p.m. Her parents will give her a five-minute warning.

- **How Well:** Details to describe the task with as much specificity as possible, to avoid misunderstandings. This is an especially important section because clear, shared expectations for both

CONTRACT

TASK

* **Who:** Lily

* **What:** Go to bed

* **When:** 8:30 p.m. Mom or Dad will give a 5-minute warning.

* **How well:** No arguing or begging to stay up. Must stay in bed until morning (can get up only to go to bathroom).

REWARD

* **Who:** Mom

* **What:** Small ceramic animals for Lily's collection

* **When:** After Lily completes the task 4 days in a row, Mom will take her to the store to pick out 1 animal

* **How much:** 1 animal

S	M	T	W	Th	F	Sat	S	M	T	W	Th	F	Sat
☺	☺	✗	☺	☺	☺	☺							

S	M	T	W	Th	F	Sat	S	M	T	W	Th	F	Sat

Sign here: _____ Lily _____ Jan 8 _____

Sign here: _____ Mom _____ Jan 8 _____

child and parent contribute to the likeliness that the contract will succeed. Not only does Lily need to be in bed at 8:30 p.m. but the contract also specifies that she must do this without arguing or begging and stay in bed until morning (she can get up only to go to the bathroom). In other words, the contract rewards positive behavior changes, and Lily knows exactly what she needs to do differently to succeed. (The chapter "Write the Contract" examines the *How Well* part of the task further.)

See the chapter "Select the Task" for a step-by-step method for identifying tasks for behavior contracts, along with common examples of tasks used in contracts.

How a Contract Describes the Reward

To describe the reward—the positive consequence your child will receive for completing the task—you fill in *Who, What, When,* and *How Much*. Here's what we mean by each, again using the example of Lily's bedtime contract.

- **Who:** The person who will determine if the task has been completed and give the reward. With Lily's contract, her mom is that person.
- **What:** The reward that you and your child have agreed to. Lily collects little ceramic animals, and the reward is a new animal for her collection.

- **When:** The time you give your child the reward. Ideally, your child gets the reward as soon as possible after they complete the task, keeping in mind that some rewards, such as going to a movie, will take place later. Lily's contract states that she will get the reward after successfully completing her task four days in a row.

- **How much:** The amount of the reward earned by completing the task. Lily gets to pick out one new ceramic animal for her collection after four consecutive successful bedtimes.

The chapter "Choose the Reward" outlines two methods for choosing rewards and examples of common rewards used in contracts with children.

FAQ: Why should my child get a reward for doing what they should be doing anyway?

Your child doesn't need a contract for tasks they're already doing regularly. Instead, consider using a contract to help motivate your child and support their success in areas where they have struggled or want to learn a new skill. Common family problems, like a child who doesn't complete chores, often lead to negative parent-child interactions. In contrast, contracts promote positive behavior changes with a spirit of cooperation among family members.

Additional Contract Elements

The task and the reward are the main parts of a contract. Here are more details about the three additional contract elements, again illustrated using the example of Lily's bedtime contract.

- **Task record:** A visual record of task completion, such as check marks next to the days of the week. Lily's mom drew a happy face on the task record each time Lily successfully went to and stayed in bed, as described in the contract.

- **Signatures:** Your signature and your child's signature. (If your child doesn't write, use an alternative such as having your child draw a circle around their name after you write it for them—a simple squiggle will also do.) Adding your names symbolizes each individual's agreement to do what the contract says and your commitment to do your best to make it work. Lily and her mom both signed the contract.

- **Official seal:** A small image that reflects your family's identity or interests in some way and signifies the contract's special status and importance. In the story "Game Suspended," teenager Lynn describes an official seal: "It's like when the post office stamps 'priority mail' on a letter and guarantees that letter will arrive on a certain day. It makes that promise more formal." Your child can draw something they like, or you can use stickers. Lily used an animal sticker for her contract.

A Disclaimer and an Invitation

Contracting won't work in every situation or for every family. No matter how well a contract is constructed and presented to a child, it may not be successful. But in many cases, a contract can help change your child's behavior and shift family dynamics from a negative tone to a positive one. That said, we believe every family who tries the techniques described in this book will benefit by gaining new insights and understanding of one another's thoughts, feelings, desires, and goals.

Next Step

To set you up for success, the next two chapters look more closely at selecting tasks and choosing rewards for contracts. For more inspiration, we also recommend reading and sharing with your child the nine stories in Part I that illustrate how contracts can work in common family scenarios.

CONTRACT

TASK	REWARD
* Who:	* Who:
* What:	* What:
* When:	* When:
* How well:	* How much:

S	M	T	W	Th	F	Sat	S	M	T	W	Th	F	Sat

S	M	T	W	Th	F	Sat	S	M	T	W	Th	F	Sat

Sign here: _____   _____

Sign here: _____   _____

**Select
the task**

**Choose the
reward**

**Write the
contract**

**Implement
the contract**

Selecting the task is the first step in creating a contract. Tasks are desirable behaviors you and your child target to do more often.

IN THIS CHAPTER, YOU'LL LEARN:

- What a task is
- Common tasks for family contracts
- Two ways to identify tasks
- Guidelines for selecting tasks

11

Select the Task

Contracts motivate a person to do something different or in a new way—for example, better, more often, or more consistently—or to do something they've never done before. With behavior contracts, that action is called the *task*. The first and foremost step in making a contract is to identify the task.

In this chapter, we're going to talk about how to select a task. You might also want to read the story "Game Suspended" with your child for more background and to show them how one family selected a task.

For the first contract, we recommend picking a task that will set your child up for success, rather than choosing the biggest or longest ongoing issue. The goal is to make contracting a pleasant experience that your child will want to repeat. You can tackle more difficult behavior challenges later. Also, don't try to change multiple behaviors with one contract. Staying focused on one doable task makes success more likely.

Successful family contracts have a range of benefits, including increasing independence and self-reliance, improving relationships with parents and siblings, encouraging helping out at home, supporting achieving personal goals, and promoting learning new skills.

Notice that all of the examples of contract tasks for family contracts shown on the following page are desirable behaviors. Of course, reducing or eliminating an undesirable behavior is one of the main reasons for making a contract. However, for the task itself, it's essential to choose a desirable behavior to replace the unwanted action.

For example, in "The Pet Menace," the task in four-year-old Maya's contract is watching the fish swim and gently petting the dog, new skills for her. If the task had been, "Do not drop blocks in the fish tank and don't pull the dog's tail," it would not have told Maya what she needed to do and taken away the chance for her to grow and proudly show off new behavior.

In "By Myself," 10-year-old Connor stalls and argues every school morning, creating a chaotic and stressful scene. The task in his contract spells out action steps required to get ready for school independently. His success results in a calm environment and fosters self-reliance. A task like "Don't cry or cause delays in the morning" would not have the same positive effects.

Common Tasks for Family Contracts

INCREASE INDEPENDENCE

- Play quietly alone
- Dress self
- Wash face and hands
- Brush teeth
- Get ready for school on time
- Pack school lunch
- Make bed
- Go to bed without a fuss
- Put away toys
- Hang up coat
- Do homework independently
- Take daily medication

GET ALONG WITH FAMILY MEMBERS

- Follow instructions without arguing
- Help younger sibling
- Share toys with sibling
- Ask sibling to play
- Ask permission before going outside

HELP OUT AT HOME

- Set table for meal
- Prepare part of meal
- Put dirty dishes in sink
- Clean bathroom
- Fold and put away laundry
- Weed garden
- Unload/load dishwasher
- Change towels or sheets
- Clean kitchen counters
- Vacuum/sweep floors
- Dust furniture
- Feed or walk pet

ACHIEVE A GOAL OR LEARN A NEW SKILL

- Try new foods
- Practice a musical instrument
- Learn a new language
- Make friends
- Exercise regularly
- Pursue a new hobby

Tip for Success: Identify a desirable task to be completed, not an undesirable behavior to decrease or stop. Working on positive behavior change builds your child's character as well as skills.

Have a Family Meeting

The first step in creating a family contract is to collaboratively identify the task. To kick off the process, call a family meeting. Many families find meeting at the table after dinner is a good time to create and later on evaluate their contracts. The first meeting is the most important. Carve out at least a half hour, with the goal of identifying a task and a reward for each person's first contract. But don't rush. If you don't finish in the first meeting, stop and continue at a second meeting on another day.

Begin the meeting by explaining to your family that contacts are a way for parents and kids to meet personal goals, and that contracts reward desirable behavior, rather than punish misdeeds or mistakes. You might show one or two of the contracts from the stories in this book as examples, or read one of the stories together. Next, explain how you're going to identify potential tasks through either an open discussion or the list-making technique we'll describe.

Open Discussion

The first option for your family meeting is to have an open discussion to select tasks. Explain that you're going to talk about how things have been going and identify tasks—actions—that each of you can do to improve family life.

Speak first and cite examples of positive tasks that family members, including yourself, could do to make things better. Remember to stay focused on desirable behaviors, rather than complaining about behaviors you don't like. Like the parents in the stories "Game Suspended," "Lynn Pitches In," and "By Myself," you may already know what task you'd like your child to address in a contract. If so, mention what you're thinking and say why you think doing the task would improve things for them and for your family.

Then give everyone else a turn to talk about their suggestions without being interrupted. It's fine to repeat or expand on ideas already mentioned. After everyone has a turn, have an open discussion about the different ideas.

MEETING GUIDELINES

Be positive. Tell your kids what's going well, not what's bothering you. Your kids already know what's bugging you. They've probably heard you tell them many times. They'll appreciate hearing what you see is going well and how they can contribute to the family in new ways.

Tip for Success: Describing positive behavior clearly and specifically is the foundation of a good contract.

Be specific. When talking about things you or others do or don't do that you would like to see changed and improved, be as *specific* as possible, rather than using general terms or labels. Being specific means explaining a task in such a way that everyone has the same understanding about the details of the task.

Here are some examples of being specific when describing behaviors and suggesting desirable behaviors.

INSTEAD OF SAYING,	YOU MIGHT SAY:
Marsha is messy.	I would like Marsha to hang up her coat and put her backpack in her room after school.
I don't like the way Brandon talks back to me.	I want Brandon to speak to me politely in a quiet tone of voice.

Reed should pitch in more.	I would like Reed to put fresh water in the dog's dish every morning and water the plants on the weekend.
Jordan doesn't help out around the house.	It helps me when Jordan puts away the groceries and takes out the trash.
I am tired of dressing Sayaka every morning.	I would like Sayaka to get dressed by herself before school.

Let the kids talk. Give each child an equal chance to speak their minds. Encourage your kids to say what they'd like to see changed. The same ground rules apply: Don't complain, and be as positive and specific as you can.

INSTEAD OF YOUR KIDS SAYING,	THEY COULD SAY:
Dad is mean to me.	I'd like Dad to let me use his tools.
Mom always says no.	I wish Mom would let me . . .
My room's a pigsty.	My room would look better if I put away my toys and picked up my clothes.

What your kids say may surprise you. Children are often able to home in on important family issues and relevant tasks. A good, open discussion usually results in pinpointing the tasks to consider for contracts.

The List-Making Approach

The list-making approach is a more structured way to identify tasks. Many families, especially those with older children who read and write, like using this step-by-step method, which uses two forms, *My Tasks* and *Your Tasks.* You can create these forms on blank sheets of paper, copy the forms in this book, or download and print the forms from contractingwithkids.com. (If you're creating your own form, divide a blank piece of paper into two columns.)

My Tasks form. Give each person a *My Tasks* form, and have everyone list things they *do now* to help the family on the left side, and write things they *could do* in the future to help on the right side. These are things you likely know you should be doing but haven't been getting done lately. Or, maybe there's something you've never done before, and you'd like to start doing it. See the examples of how 14-year-old Charlotte and her mom completed their forms.

Your Tasks form. After each family member completes a *My Tasks* form, give everyone a *Your Tasks* form and follow these steps to complete it. You fill out this form for everyone else at the meeting, but not for yourself. See the examples of how the other family members completed the *Your Tasks* forms for Derek and Dad.

- In the left column, write at the top "Things [your name] does to help our family."

- In the right column, write at the top "Other ways [your name] could help."

- Pass your form to someone else.

Each person in the family will fill in your form, and you'll fill in everyone else's form.

- In the left column, list the things you recognize that person does now to help your family.

- In the right column, list ways you think that person could help more.

- Pass each form from one person to another until everyone else has written on each other's forms.

A good rule is that everyone should write at least one thing on each side of everyone else's *Your Tasks* form.

The examples show what eight-year-old Derek's mother, father, and older sister wrote on Derek's *Your Tasks* form and what the list for Derek's dad looked like this after his wife and two children completed it.

MY TASKS: Charlotte

THINGS I DO TO HELP MY FAMILY

- Feed the dogs

- Empty the dishwasher and put everything away

- Babysit Lana sometimes

- Help Dad with the laundry

OTHER WAYS I COULD HELP MY FAMILY AND MYSELF

- Be on time for dinner

- Write down my soccer practices and games in the family calendar

- Hang up my coat and put my backpack in my room when I come home

- Practice the piano

MY TASKS: Mom

THINGS I DO TO HELP MY FAMILY

- Go to work

- Cook dinner three nights a week

- Drive Charlotte to soccer practice and games

- Plan vacations

- Pay the bills

OTHER WAYS I COULD HELP MY FAMILY AND MYSELF

- Teach Charlotte to play the guitar

- Cut back on checking social media and read more

- Go to the pool more with the kids

- Help in the garden

YOUR TASKS: Derek

WHAT Derek	OTHER WAYS Derek
DOES TO HELP OUR FAMILY	**COULD HELP**

WHAT Derek

DOES TO HELP OUR FAMILY

- Sweeps and vacuums when asked
- Makes his bed
- Plays board games with Brianna
- Takes the recycling bin to the curb
- Tells funny jokes and makes us laugh
- Gets ready for school on time

OTHER WAYS Derek

COULD HELP

- Put his dirty clothes in the hamper
- Do homework without reminders
- Clear off and clean table after dinner
- Pack his lunch the night before

YOUR TASKS: Dad

WHAT
Dad

DOES TO HELP OUR FAMILY

- Goes to work

- Helps kids with homework

- Makes breakfast on weekends

- Plants and tends the garden

- Mails birthday cards to out-of-town family

OTHER WAYS
Dad

COULD HELP

- Clean the basement and garage

- Teach me to use the waffle iron

- Shoot hoops with me more

- Show everyone what to do when the Internet goes down so we can fix it if Dad's not home

- Teach me to draw cartoons

Tip for Success: Pick a task for your child's first contract that they're likely to be successful with. You can tackle more difficult behavior challenges later on.

When completing the *Your Tasks* form for your child, list more positive behaviors your child is doing now than behaviors you'd like your child to do in the future. This is an opportunity to let your child know you notice and appreciate their current efforts.

Choose the First Task

Have everyone look at their two tasks forms closely. Go around the table and help each person decide which task is the *most important* for their first contract. Asking these questions can help decide which task to choose:

- Would this person be a better family member if they did this task?

- Would our family as a whole be happier and better off if they did this task?

- Is this task something the person can do independently? (If not, can we make the task more doable?)

If the answer to these questions is yes, it's probably an important task. Contracts work best when all the people who sign them agree that the task is important. In the chapter "Write the Contract," we'll explain how to specify the *How Well* details of the task.

Next Step

After you've selected a task for everyone's first contract, it's time for the fun part. In the next chapter, you'll choose the reward for each contract.

HOW TO MAKE A CONTRACT

**Select
the task**

**Choose the
reward**

**Write the
contract**

**Implement
the contract**

Choosing the reward is the second step in creating a contract. Rewards are a proven way to effect behavior change in a positive way.

IN THIS CHAPTER, YOU'LL LEARN:

- The purpose of rewards
- Common rewards for family contracts
- Two ways to identify rewards
- Guidelines for choosing a reward

12

Choose the Reward

Selecting the task, as described in the previous chapter, is the first step in creating a contract with your child. The second step is choosing a reward that will motivate them to do the task. To be effective, rewards don't have to be (and shouldn't be) expensive, elaborate, or time-consuming. They can be low-cost items, or better still, activities or outings you can enjoy together. Sometimes the actual reward is less important to your child than the fact that you are willing to provide a positive consequence for their behavior, rather than taking a punitive approach.

A reward can jump-start behavior change and boost your child's sense of accomplishment and satisfaction. When your child experiences the natural rewards of success and accomplishment, as they often do, the contract may no longer be necessary.

Family contracts often include rewards such as those in the following lists.

Common Rewards for Family Contracts

AT-HOME ACTIVITIES

- Play video games
- Get extra bedtime story
- Paint or draw
- Stay up late on weekend
- Have friend sleep over
- Play card or board game
- Do jigsaw puzzle
- Cook something special
- Order out from favorite restaurant
- Make friendship bracelet
- Make slime

FAMILY OUTINGS

- Visit zoo
- Picnic in park
- Go to playground
- Visit library
- Ride on bike trail
- Have campfire
- Walk at night with flashlights
- Go to movies
- Go out for pizza
- Take hike

SPECIAL TREATS

- Choose ice cream flavor
- Breakfast in bed
- Stickers
- Surprise from grab bag
- No-chores-day ticket
- Pick what's for dinner
- Pancake breakfast
- Money
- Doll clothes
- Hobby materials
- Cards for collection
- Building kits like Lego
- Toy cars
- Board games
- Child-safe handstamp
- Extra screen time
- TV show or movie
- Art supplies
- Book or magazine
- New app

Two Ways to Identify Rewards

In the previous chapter, we recommended holding a family meeting to collaboratively pick a task for the contract. Once you agree on a task, you can use the same family meeting format to choose a reward together. You might show one or two of the contracts from the stories in this book as examples. Next, explain how you're going to identify potential rewards through either an open discussion or the list-making technique we describe.

Open Discussion

An open discussion is a simple and straightforward approach to choosing rewards that works in most cases. Invite your child to suggest ideas. For your part, think about the activities, outings, and things your child likes. Draw on this knowledge to suggest ideas for rewards. In the stories "Game Suspended" and "Lynn Pitches In," parents suggest the rewards, and their kids readily embrace them.

The reward can also be a menu of options from which your child chooses one each time they earn a reward. In the "Making Friends" story, for example, Connor and his mom decide that each day he completes the task on his contract he can choose one from a list of three different activities or special treats.

An effective reward for some tasks is access to the activity your child consistently does instead of the desired task. In "The Number

FAQ: Would a penalty for failing to complete the task make a contract more effective?

We don't recommend punitive consequences for failing to do the task. Carrying out a penalty often requires negative parent-child interactions, which produce undesirable outcomes such as arguing, anxiety about receiving the penalty, and/or complete withdrawal from the contract. Research shows reward-only contracts to be as effective as contracts with penalties, and both children and adults prefer the reward-only approach.

Problem" story, fourth-grader Perry was having trouble understanding fractions. Perry told his parents he wanted to do better in math but instead of studying he played video games. Perry works out a contract with a task of solving ten new problems each weeknight. Once he finishes the problems, he is rewarded with permission to play video games for up to an hour until his bedtime. This reward acts as an incentive for Perry to tackle the math problems right after dinner.

The List-Making Approach

The list-making approach is a more structured way to identify rewards. Many families, especially those with older children who read, like this step-by-step method. Each family member fills out a

My Rewards form. (You can write *My Rewards* lists on blank sheets of paper, copy the form from this book, or download and print the form from contractingwithkids.com.)

On the form, have your child list things they'd enjoy as a reward for completing the task. The list can be divided into categories such as activities, outings, and special treats.

As an example, we've shown how 14-year-old Charlotte completed her *My Rewards* form. For another example, look at the list of rewards Charlotte's dad made.

Go around the table and have each family member suggest a reward from their list that they would like to receive for doing the task in their contract. Then talk about each person's choice. Kids will sometimes test their parents by including expensive or outlandish items on their rewards list. They know those things aren't possible, so just smile or laugh and say, "Wouldn't that be nice! Now, let's look at this other item that's more reasonable."

Guidelines for Selecting Rewards

The following questions can help you decide what to choose as the reward:

- Is my child enthusiastic about this reward? You want your child's first contract to be successful, so pick a reward that's a bit special. Don't give away the store, but don't be stingy either.

MY REWARDS: Charlotte

AT-HOME ACTIVITIES

- Listen to music
- Play online word games
- Do Sudoku puzzles
- Run on the treadmill

SPECIAL TREATS/ ITEMS

- New hoodie
- Pillows for my bedroom
- New running shoes
- Sudoku puzzle books

COMMUNITY ACTIVITIES

- Go out for pizza
- Go bowling
- Ride the new bike trail
- Watch a Netflix movie

OTHER

- More time to text my friends
- Have a friend sleep over
- Skip emptying the dishwasher some days

MY REWARDS: Dad

MY FAVORITE ACTIVITIES, THINGS, AND SPECIAL TREATS

- Go out to dinner with Mom

- Play trivia with my friends on Tuesday night

- Go bowling with Charlotte

- Go to movies with the kids

- Watch old movies at home

- Read the Sunday paper without getting interrupted

- Buy favorite coffee beans

- Is the reward reasonable? Does it fit the task? The reward needs to be fair, not too big and not too small relative to the effort the task involves. We'll talk about how to decide the *How Much* part of the reward in the next chapter, "Write the Contract."

- Can you easily give the reward each time your child completes the task? Rewards are most effective when received immediately or soon after the task. This is especially true for a child's first contract. We'll talk about how to decide when to give the reward in the next chapter, "Write the Contract," and how to record the details in the contract.

- Are you willing to withhold the reward if the task isn't completed? If your child doesn't complete the task, they don't get the reward. If you don't follow this rule and give in to your child's whining or begging, you will be rewarding and reinforcing those undesired behaviors instead of the desired task on the contract.

Next Step

Once you've selected the task and the reward, it's time to incorporate them into the contract, which we cover in the next chapter, "Write the Contract."

MY REWARDS:

AT-HOME ACTIVITIES

-
-
-
-

SPECIAL TREATS/ITEMS

-
-
-
-

COMMUNITY ACTIVITIES

-
-
-
-

OTHER

-
-
-
-

**Select
the task** **Choose the
reward** **Write the
contract** **Implement
the contract**

Writing the contract is the third step in contracting. This step combines the task and reward into an if-then relationship.

IN THIS CHAPTER, YOU'LL LEARN HOW TO

- Write the task details

- Write the reward details

- Create a task record

- Review, sign, and seal the contract

13

Write the Contract

Family contracts can be written in a variety of ways, but we recommend using a standard format to ensure that all key components are included. You can copy contract forms from this book or download and print them from contractingwithkids.com.

At this point, you've selected a task and chosen a reward—the first two steps in creating a contract. In the third step, writing a contract, you and your child will discuss, negotiate, and record specific details that clearly describe the task and reward.

FAQ: Why should I negotiate with my child?

The more your child feels like a partner in the contract, the more likely it is to succeed. Listening to your child's input and incorporating their suggestions shows you respect their opinions, ideas, and concerns. They're also likely to bring up issues that you might not have considered. Contracting is more likely to be successful when you listen, are open to negotiating, and are committed to reaching a mutually acceptable agreement.

To write the contract, start with a blank contract form and fill out the task details:

- **Who:** Write the name of the person who will do the task.

- **What:** Write a brief descriptive name for the task.

Now comes the time to determine *when* the task should be done, *how well* it has to be done, and whether any exceptions will be allowed.

When should the task be completed?

Almost every contract has a time element attached to it. Here are some questions to think about: Should the task be done every day, once a week, or a minimum number of times each day or week? Is it important that the task be started and/or completed at specific times? Does the task need to be carried out over a period of time? In "The Pet Menace," Maya had to "be good to the pets" from the time she got home from preschool until dinner, and again from after dinner until her bedtime.

Can the task be done whenever your child wants to do it as long as the task is completed by a certain day or time? If the task is "practice the piano" four times per week, for example, the contract might say your child can choose to practice on any four days during the week.

Some examples of when tasks have to be completed are illustrated in the following contracts:

- Perry's contract in "The Number Problem" said he'd spend a half hour solving fraction problems after dinner.

- Lynn's contract in "Lynn Pitches In" stated she'd start to prepare dinner by 4:30 p.m. Monday through Friday.

- Connor's contract in "By Myself" specified that he had to be ready for the bus by 7:45 a.m. each school day.

Once you and your child have discussed and determined when the task must be completed, write the requirements next to *When* on the contract.

If the contract will be in effect for only a given period of time, write that on the contract along with the precise time frame. For example, Lynn's contract with her mother was for three weeks.

How well must the task be completed?

The *How Well* part of the contract is intended to prevent disagreements about whether or not the task has been completed. It's essential that everyone understands and agrees on this component. Lack of clarity on what completing the task means is a major reason contracts fail.

In the stories "Game Suspended" and "Loopholes," it was important for the family to be specific about Jeff's room-cleaning contract. Jeff's first contract didn't work until he and his dad determined *exactly* what a "cleaned-up" bedroom looked like. Jeff and his dad talked about how to fix the contract and came up with this amended list:

- Pick up all clothes off floor, bed, desk, and chair. Clothes must be put away in dresser or hung up in closet.

- Put guitar in case and models and books on shelves.

- Clear top of desk. Put pencils in mug on desk and homework in backpack.

- Make bed.

Jeff could then use the contract as a checklist of what he needed to do. Here are some additional examples of defining how well the task must be done:

- Perry's revised contract in "The Number Problem" said he had to solve ten new fraction problems correctly.

- Connor's contract in "By Myself" required him to complete the four steps of his "get ready for school" task. His mother took photos showing Connor doing each step and attached them to the contract.

- Lynn's task of giving "cooking lessons for Jeff" in "Siblings United" specified that she would explain each recipe step and let Jeff try to do it.

Once you and your child have discussed and determined how well the task must be completed, write those requirements next to *How Well* on the contract.

Are there any exceptions to task requirements?

The last thing to consider when defining the task are exceptions. Some tasks must be done every day—tasks like feeding the cat, cooking dinner for a hungry family, or going to bed on time. But your child might skip other tasks now and then without losing his reward—tasks like practicing a musical instrument, making the bed, or helping another family member work on a special project.

If you're going to allow exceptions, it's better to decide at the outset and write them into the contract in advance, so no one can argue about it later. This is where negotiation is often required.

In the story "Loopholes," Jeff asked his dad, "What if I miss one day? Does that mean I won't get the reward? So we won't spend special time together on Saturday?"

His dad defined an exception by saying, "Let's write that you can miss one day a week and still earn the reward. But just one day—no more." They then wrote on the contract that Jeff could miss one day each week without losing his reward.

Lynn could skip preparing dinner one night over the three weeks of her time-limited contract with her mom and still get her reward.

Once you and your child have discussed and determined whether exceptions will be permitted, write the details next to *When* or *How Well* on the contract.

This chart shows how the Fields family specified *When, How Well,* and *Exceptions* for each family member's tasks: nine-year-old Zack to play with his five-year-old sister, Zelda; teenager Zora to unload and load the dishwasher; Dad to spend more time with Zora; and Mom to exercise more.

Tip for Success: Set reasonable expectations your child can meet. Don't write a contract where one bad day or event eliminates your child's chance of earning the reward. Including exceptions in the contract in advance reflects that in real life no one is perfect, and that's okay.

TASK	WHEN	HOW WELL	EXCEPTIONS
Zack: Play with Zelda	Weekdays: • Before or after dinner • Saturday and Sunday: Twice each day	Any one or combination of these activities for 15 minutes: • Play a game with Zelda • Read to Zelda • Build blocks with Zelda • Show Zelda how to write her name and numbers 1 to 10	Can miss one weekday
Zora: Unload and load dishwasher	• Monday to Friday • Unload by 5 p.m. • Load by 30 minutes after dinner	• Unload: Put all clean dishes away • Load: Put all dirty dinner dishes in dishwasher	Can skip task if Zora: • Goes to friend's house for dinner • Has test or school project due the next day
Dad: Spend more time with Zora	Every day	Do any two of these with Zora for at least 10 minutes each: • Talk about school or outside activities • Ask her what she thinks about a current event • Invite her to do something like taking a walk • Play a video game with her	• Can do one task option, instead of two, if it lasts at least 20 minutes • Zora can request a wild-card activity, but Dad can veto
Mom: Exercise	Three days per week	Do any one of these: • Yoga (20 min) • Run (1 mile) • Stationary bike (20 min) • Online Pilates class	None

Write the Reward Details

A good contract is as specific about the reward as it is about the task.

WHO GIVES THE REWARD AND WHAT IS IT?

Begin by putting the person's name who will provide the reward next to *Who* and writing a description of the reward next to *What*. Most contracts specify one reward, but you can also list a menu of rewards and then allow your child to choose one after completing the task each time. This option gives your child ongoing self-agency to make a choice. The variety can also prevent your child from growing tired of the same reward. For example, in "Making Friends," each day Connor completed his "talk to another student" task at school, he could choose from three different rewards at home.

WHEN WILL THE REWARD BE GIVEN?

Next comes specifying *When* the reward will be given. The reward is always delivered after the task has been completed. If possible, the child should receive the reward immediately after doing the task. In "The Number Problem," as soon as Perry solved ten problems he could start playing video games. In "The Pet Menace," immediately after Maya had been nice to the pets for the required amount of time, her older sister or one of her parents would read her a story.

Some contracts require the task to be completed a certain number of times before the reward is earned. In the chapter "Picture Contracts for Nonreaders," Josh's reward of making one of his favorite desserts with his dad would come after he set the table five times. In the chapter "What Is Contracting?" Lily had to go to bed and follow the contract requirements four days in a row to earn her reward.

Some rewards can be provided only at specific times. For example, in "Game Suspended," Jeff's reward of special activities with his dad would be on Saturdays.

Here are some examples of contracts in which the reward is not given immediately following the task:

- In "Lynn Pitches In," Lynn's reward of going to the flea market with her mom to pick out a desk was at the end of the month.

- In "By Myself," Connor received one small Lego character after school each day he got ready for school and followed the contract requirements in the morning.

- In "Now It's Your Turn, Mom and Dad," Lynn and Jeff's parents could pick a weekend night to receive their reward of a special dinner cooked by their kids.

HOW MUCH REWARD?

It's very important that everyone involved with the contract perceives the reward and the amount of the reward in relation to the task as *fair*. A fair reward should be big enough to give your child something to look forward to while doing the task, but it shouldn't be too big, elaborate, or expensive. For example, Don and his parents agreed that if he did the dishes four times a week, he could have a friend over for dinner on Sunday. This seemed *fair* to all of them. Having his entire class over for a party on Saturday would be an example of a reward too outsized for the task.

Remember, everyone who signs the contract must agree that the reward is fair. Here are some examples of fair and unfair rewards.

TASK	FAIR REWARD	UNFAIR REWARD
Do homework every night	One hour of screen time	10 minutes of screen time (too small)
Practice clarinet for 30 minutes three times per week	Order pizza every two weeks	Get pizza every night you practice (too big)
Fold the laundry twice a week	Go to a movie after four successful weeks	Go to a movie in the next couple of months (too small, distant, and vague)
Turn off electronic device within five minutes of being asked	30 minutes of extra screen time the next day	30 minutes of extra screen time on the weekend (too small and distant)

> **Tip for Success:** Build in bonuses for completing the task a certain number of consecutive times or over an extended period.

BONUS REWARDS

The opportunity to earn bonus rewards can make a contract even more motivating for your child. For example, in "By Myself," each morning Connor successfully got himself ready for school, he earned a small Lego character. For a perfect week, he received an additional character as a bonus. Any bonus requirements should be detailed in the contract.

The chart on the following page shows how the Fields family specified the reward, when it would be given, and how much the reward would be for each of their contract tasks.

TASK	REWARD	WHEN	HOW MUCH
Zack: Play with Zelda	• Extra screen time • Mom's "secret ingredient" popcorn • Puzzle pieces • Bonus: Have friend sleep over	• Daily after dinner • Bonus after meeting contract for two weeks	Daily choose one: • 10 minutes extra screen time • Small bowl of popcorn • 2 puzzle pieces for family puzzle (when puzzle is complete, family will take a weekend trip) Bonus: Sleepover comes with movie choice and morning smoothies
Zora: Unload and load dishwasher	Choose my favorite meal for dinner	On Sunday	Every two weeks
Dad: Spend more time with Zora	I don't need a special reward. Time with Zora will be reward enough.	Daily	Go fishing, just Zora and me
Mom: Exercise	• Read for fun • Watch a show • Bonus: Dinner out with a friend	Daily: After kids are in bed Bonus: After two weeks of meeting contract	Daily choose one: • Read 1 hour • Watch hour-long episode Bonus: casual restaurant

Create a Task Record

Marking task completions on the contract—for instance, with check marks, stars, or stickers—provides ongoing positive visual feedback to your child, and reminds you to recognize and praise your child's improved behavior. Each morning after Lily had a successful bedtime, her mom praised her accomplishment and marked a smiley face on the task record of her contract. This made it easy for Lily to see her progress completing the task four days in a row to earn her reward, and for her mom to evaluate how the contract was going daily and over a longer period of time.

Most of the time, the task record can be included directly on the contract, as shown by the examples in this book. Alternatively, the task record can be on a separate sheet of paper to give more space to record progress.

Tip for Success: Self-inking stamps and stickers are a fun way to mark colorful stars, happy faces, or other positive symbols on your child's task record. Colored markers, pens, and crayons work just as well for handwritten symbols, such as check marks, or to fill in blank shapes such as a row of circles.

Review, Sign, and Seal the Contract

Now that you've written the task and reward details and constructed a task record, the contract is ready for signing. Before signing it, you and your child should review the contract to be sure it spells out everything specifically and that you both agree with what it says.

The questions in the checklist below will help you determine if you're ready to finalize the terms of the contract. When a contract is complete and clear, you and your child will be able to answer each question with a confident yes. If you can't answer yes to one or more of these questions, explore why and discuss how to address the concern.

Contract Checklist

- Is the task important for you and your family?
  ___ Yes ___ No/Not Sure

- Does everyone understand how well the task must be performed?
  ___ Yes ___ No/Not Sure

- Is it clear when the task must be done?
  ___ Yes ___ No/Not Sure

- Are there any exceptions? If so, are they clear?
  ___ Yes ___ No/Not Sure

- Is the reward fair?
  ___ Yes ___ No/Not Sure

- Is it clear how the task record works and who will mark it?
  ___ Yes ___ No/Not Sure

Once you can answer yes to all of these questions, it's time for the all-important contract signing. By putting their names on the contract, each person acknowledges the task is important, the reward is fair, and the contract will be upheld as written. A child who does not write can make a symbol such as a scribble or an X, or a parent or sibling can write the child's name and have them circle it.

Attach your family's official seal, and the contract is ready to go. For examples of official seals, see the sample contracts in this book and at contractingwithkids.com.

Next Step

In the next chapter, we'll offer suggestions for implementing the contract and evaluating its effects on your child's behavior and your family's well-being.

HOW TO MAKE A CONTRACT

Select the task

Choose the reward

Write the contract

Implement the contract

Now that you've written your contract, the next step is putting it into practice.

IN THIS CHAPTER, YOU'LL LEARN HOW TO

- Get contracts off to a good start

- Troubleshoot contracts

- Evaluate contracts

- Fade and end contracts

14

Implement the Contract

By the time you've reached this part of the book, it's likely you've invested a good bit of time and consideration into developing a contract with your child. Now it's time to put the contract into action.

Get Your Contract Off to a Good Start

When implementing a contract, these guidelines can help maximize its chance of success.

Show enthusiasm about starting the contract. Let your child know that you're really pleased they are trying the contract and you anticipate that it will be fun to work together toward a goal.

Depending on your child's age and the task, you might say things like:

- "I'm really excited about trying this contract with you. I know you can do it."

- "I told Grandma about your contract, and she's looking forward to seeing it when she visits next week."

- "I'm happy that we're working on this as a team."

Let the contract do the work. Don't prompt your child to do the task on the contract. One of the benefits of having a written contract is eliminating the need for constantly reminding, nagging, pleading, or directing your child. This is a chance to trust your child to try a new approach.

Praise your child for completing the task. Your praise is one of the most powerful tools for changing your child's behavior. When your child does the task, giving sincere praise and specific feedback will be much more effective than reprimands and punishments for failing to do it.

Praise is most effective when it is immediate and specific. Praise your child's behavior as soon as possible after they have completed the task. Saying "good job" is positive but doesn't pinpoint exactly what your child has done to warrant your positive feedback. If you say this common phrase too often, it's likely to lose its impact.

Here are some examples of behavior-specific praise:

- "Your bedroom looks so nice and neat. It's great that you can work on your projects now that your desk has clear space."

- "It must feel good to have solved so many math problems correctly. That should help you feel more confident for your next math quiz."

- "I'm happy that you're not so rushed in the mornings. Now we can relax and enjoy breakfast together before school."

- "Thanks for your help with the dishes. It gives me a break after a long day at work."

Nonverbal feedback, such as hugs, high fives, and fist bumps, is also an effective way to show your child how proud you are of their accomplishments.

Reward only a successfully completed task. If your child doesn't do the task as required by the contract, don't lecture or scold. If your child asks why they're not getting the reward, refer to the contract using a neutral tone of voice, and encourage them to complete the task at the next opportunity.

Troubleshooting Contracts

Contracts often require some adjustments once implemented. If you run into a snag, the contract may just need some small changes to make the task more explicit or the reward more motivating to your child.

In "Game Suspended," Jeff's first contract with his dad didn't work because they had different ideas of what a cleaned-up bedroom looks like. After Jeff and his dad discussed their expectations, agreed on the task details, and revised the contract in "Loopholes," it was successful.

Contracts that expect too much behavior change right away often fail. In "The Pet Menace," four-year-old Maya's contract initially required her

Tip for Success: If a contract isn't working, change it. Even the most thoughtfully planned and well-written contracts often need fine-tuning to be effective.

to be good to the pets from the time she arrived home from preschool in the afternoon until her bedtime. Maya wanted to make her contract, but that period of time was too long for her.

Even when your child consistently completes the task, a contract can still fail. In "The Number Problem," Perry studied math for a half hour as his contract stated, but his math skills didn't improve. Changing the task to "solve ten fraction problems" helped Perry attain his goal of doing better in his math class.

Following the examples of the families in this book, if things don't work as planned with your contract, don't throw in the towel. Troubleshoot, revise, and try again. Most problems with contracts are due to one of the reasons listed in the following chart. If a problem and possible reason ring true to your situation, these possible solutions may help.

PROBLEM	POSSIBLE REASON	POSSIBLE SOLUTIONS
You and your child disagree on whether the task is completed.	• The task is not clearly specified.	• See the chapter "Write the Contract." • Discuss, negotiate, and rewrite the *When* and *How Well* task parts of the contract.

Your child doesn't meet the task requirements.	• Your child doesn't understand the task. • The task is not clearly specified. • The task is too difficult for your child's current ability.	• Demonstrate the task, watch your child do it, and give feedback. • Praise your child's attempts. • Provide visual prompts such as photos or audio aids like a timer app (see Resources). • Revise task details in the contract. • Change the task requirements. • Consider if you're judging their attempts fairly. Ask yourself: Are your child's efforts "good enough" for their current ability?
Your child never attempts the task.	• Your child forgot. • The reward doesn't provide sufficient motivation. • Your child never wanted or intended to do the contract.	• Put the contract in a prominent place as a reminder. • Teach your child to use a timer or app as a prompt. • Discuss changing the reward with your child (see the chapter "Choose the Reward"). • Ask your child why they're not attempting the task after signing the contract. Listen to their answer and see if you can troubleshoot together. • See the chapter "If Your Child Won't Try Contracting."

PROBLEM	POSSIBLE REASON	POSSIBLE SOLUTIONS
Your child makes negative statements about the contract.	• Your child is in the habit of arguing and ignoring your instructions.	• See the chapter "If Your Child Won't Try Contracting."
After completing the task and receiving the reward once or twice, your child loses interest.	• Your child may want more of your attention. • The reward no longer motivates your child.	• Pay more attention to each task completion and give specific praise (see tips on praise on page 164). • Let your child choose from a menu of rewards. • Give a bonus reward for consecutive task completions, such as a perfect week.
Your child reliably completes the task, but the underlying problem isn't resolved.	• Contract may have focused on the wrong task (e.g., when Perry studied fractions for a half hour, rather than solving ten problems with fractions).	• Discuss why the contract was written. Revisit what problem it was meant to solve and the goal it was meant to achieve. • If the task doesn't directly help solve the problem or reach the goal, select another task that will.
The contract "works" but you or your child aren't happy with it.	• The contract requires too much work. • The reward isn't fun for your child.	• Revisit the entire contracting process, see chapters "Select the Task," "Choose the Reward," and "Write the Contract."

Evaluating Contracts

Once you implement the contract, do any troubleshooting, and see that your child is doing the task, monitor closely and frequently reevaluate the process both objectively and subjectively. Here are some suggestions:

Look at your child's behavior. The task record is a visible representation of your child's actions and offers an objective tool to evaluate the contract's success in terms of changed behavior. Does the task record show that your child is consistently completing the task?

Also, think through the following questions. Then, share your thoughts with and get feedback from your child.

Ask yourself:

- Did your child complete the task correctly in the set time period?

- Has the behavior improved, even a small amount, compared to before the contract was implemented?

- Did your child earn the reward, and did you give it to them in a timely manner?

If the answers are yes, the contract is a success at its most basic level.

Consider each family member's perspective. While a contract may result in the desired behavior change, that's not the only measure of success. It's also important to consider how each participant feels about the contracting process.

Ask yourself:

- Does your child feel good about completing the task?

- Does your child enjoy the reward?

- Is contracting having a positive effect on your relationship with your child?

- Are you comfortable using contracting?

If answers to any of the above questions are no, work with your child to see if you can tweak the contract and implement it in a way that makes it both more effective and enjoyable for all family members.

If appropriate, call a family meeting to hear different perspectives. Share the task record, as well as your personal assessment of how things are going. Ask your child and other family members, if applicable:

- How do you think the contract is going?

- Do you have any suggestions for improving it?

Use the troubleshooting chart in this chapter and refer back to previous chapters or relevant stories to direct the conversation.

Continue to fine-tune together. When you and your child agree on any changes, record them on the original contract and initial the changes. If the changes are significant, draw up a new contract.

Fading and Ending Contracts

In most cases, contracts are not designed to be in place permanently. Contracting is a transitional tool to get positive behaviors going until they become part of your child's routine.

Some contracts can be time-limited from the start, while others can be gradually faded out. Research has shown the following progression to be an effective way to fade out contracts.

- **You manage the task and the reward.** You work with your child to identify and specify the task and reward. You monitor and record your child's performance on the task record. You deliver the reward.

- **Your child monitors the task. You deliver the reward.** You teach your child to monitor their own task performance by first monitoring it jointly. Once your child's monitoring is accurate, allow your child to self-monitor. When your child tells you the task is completed, you provide the reward.

- **Your child manages the task and the reward.** Your child determines when the task is complete and accesses their own reward, possibly choosing from a reward menu.

- **Your child completes the task without a reward.** Your child no longer needs a reward to be motivated to complete the task. The positive behavior change has become routine.

- **Your child can create a self-contract for a new task, if desired.** When the original contract wraps up, your child might enjoy the opportunity to develop a self-contract in which they identify a new task and way to reward themselves. Depending on your child's age and skill level, they might even manage the entire contracting process independently.

Keep Collaborating

Your child might take to contracting right away or like it once you've refined what you're doing. It's normal to need to refine contracts once you try them out, and we encourage you to collaboratively troubleshoot with your child. If your child remains uncomfortable with contracting, see Resources for other positive parenting strategies.

Even if contracting doesn't solve the initial problem, give your child props for trying a new approach. Simply being involved in the contracting process will help your child learn a range of skills, including problem-solving, negotiation, and self-advocacy.

We wish you and your family many successful contracts. It would mean the world to us if *Let's Make a Contract* helps you change your child's behavior in a positive way and contributes to improved relationships in your family.

Next Step

The final two chapters address special situations: how to create picture contracts for nonreaders and what to do if your child doesn't want to try contracting. If neither situation applies, you're good to go.

HOW TO MAKE A CONTRACT

Select the task

Choose the reward

Write the contract

Implement the contract

Contracts don't have to be written with words. Children who don't read can also benefit from contracts.

IN THIS CHAPTER, YOU'LL LEARN:

- How to make a picture contract

15

Picture Contracts for Nonreaders

Even though contracts are usually written in words, phrases, or short sentences, you can use pictures or symbols to represent the task and the reward if your child does not read—or if your child prefers to use pictures.

Nonreaders for whom picture contracts can be effective include:

- Preschoolers (three to five years old), like Maya in "The Pet Menace"

- Children in elementary school with limited reading and writing skills

- Older children with disabilities who lack reading skills but can understand the if-then relationship between the task and reward on a contract, which is "If I do this, then I will get that."

Let's take a look at a picture contract developed for Josh, a nonreader with limited written word recognition skills who understands oral instructions.

CONTRACT

TASK	REWARD

Sign here: *Josh* Feb 14

Sign here: *Dad* Feb 14

Task

In this example, Josh's task is setting the table. Photos illustrate the task parts of the contract:

- *Who* and *What:* A photo shows Josh setting the table.

- *When*: An image of a clockface displays the time he should start the task in order for it to be completed on time.

- *How Well:* A photo shows a placemat with a plate, silverware, glass, and napkin in the proper positions. Josh can verify that he's done the task correctly by comparing where he placed each item with what the photo shows.

Reward

In this example, the reward is Josh gets to make a dessert with Dad. Photos illustrate the reward parts of the contract:

- *Who* and *What:* A photo shows Josh and his father baking cookies. Right below are photos of the three other desserts Josh can choose to make with his dad.

- *When:* A row of five empty circles on the contract represents the number of days until Josh will receive the reward. Each day after Josh sets the table, his dad or mom gives him a sticker in the shape of a circle, which he puts over one of the empty circles.

Tip for Success: A successful first contract is especially important to help nonreaders understand the if-then relationship between the task and the reward. Even though Josh had to set the table for five nights before he could make a special dessert with his dad, receiving a sticker and attaching it to his contract each time he sets the table gives him an immediate positive consequence for completing the task.

When all five circles are covered with a sticker, Josh gets to choose one of four different desserts to make with his dad.

- In addition to showing when the reward will be earned, the five circles double as a task record. Each time Josh places a sticker on the contract he and his parents can see his progress.

- *How Much:* Photos of four desserts show Josh the dessert menu options from which he can choose.

Josh chose an image of a stand mixer as the official seal for his contract.

Images for Picture Contracts

When using only pictures or drawings instead of written words to illustrate each part of the contract, the primary goal is to find or create images that your child understands. Their meaning should be clear and their content as specific as possible. Image sources may include any one or a combination of the following:

Personalized photos. Take pictures of your child that correspond to the task and reward parts of the contract, such as *What* doing the task looks like (for example, making the bed) and *How Well* a task needs to be done (photo of a neatly made bed). In "By Myself," Connor's mother took photos of him doing each step of his "get ready for school" task. In the "The Pet Menace," a photo of three of Maya's favorite books represented the reward of having a story read to her.

Pictures from online sources or print publications. If you're searching for images online, make your search as specific as possible by including key words for the setting, such as "bedroom," where the task will be performed in addition to words describing the task and reward items. In Maya's contract, part of her "be nice to the pets" task was depicted by a picture of a girl playing happily with a dog, which her family found in a pet food ad in a magazine.

Hand-drawn images. If your child or another member of the family likes to draw, they can illustrate the contract parts. These sketches don't have to be works of art, just clear enough to communicate what the task and reward are. To illustrate "watch the fish swim instead of bothering them," Maya's sister drew a picture of a girl looking at fish swimming in a tank with big smiles on their faces.

Symbols or icons. Josh's contract had five circles to represent that he needed to complete the task for five days to earn the reward.

Visual task record. Your child can use visual rather than numerical cues to record completed tasks. Josh using stickers to fill in the circles each time he completed his task is an example of a visual task record. His parents alternatively could have had him color in five circles leading to a picture of the reward.

Ways to Represent Time

Many contracts involve a time factor. Here are some visual ways to illustrate time with images rather than words:

- **Clock face.** Even if your child doesn't tell time, you can use the image of a clockface to show what a clock looks like at relevant times. For example, if your child can have screen time from 7:00 p.m. to 8:00 p.m. as a reward, draw a picture of the face of a clock set at 7:00 p.m. and a second clock face showing 8:00 p.m. Hang or place a nondigital clock with easily read numbers nearby for your child to refer to. Similarly, you can use the image of a digital clock, if that would be more familiar to your child.

- **Time of day.** You can illustrate a task that must start or be completed at a certain time of day, for example, a sun rising to indicate when your child gets up in the morning or a school bus to indicate the time they must be ready to leave.

- **Timer.** If the task or reward has a time frame attached to it, such as reading for 30 minutes as the task and playing a computer learning game for 30 minutes as the reward, your family can use a manual kitchen timer. Demonstrate how to set the timer (you can mark the exact task and rewards times with tape or a sticker) and explain that the sound signals the end of the time. Alternatively, you could teach your child to use one of many free apps for tablets and smartphones that help children keep track of time (see Resources).

Make Your Own Picture Contract

Here are instructions for making picture contracts.

- **Plan the activity.** Before you start, consider how you can involve your child in creating the contract and make it a fun activity. Pick a time that's generally good for you and your child—when you don't have to rush and no one is hungry or tired.

- **Divide space in half.** You can use a sheet of paper, tape several sheets together, or use poster board, depending on how much space you need for the pictures. The left side will show the task. The right side will show the reward.

- **Attach a picture on the left side to illustrate the task.** It should show your child (*Who*) doing the task (*What*) in a way that your child will best understand.

- **Attach a picture on the right side to illustrate the reward.** Depending on what the reward is, the picture might show an object or your child enjoying an activity. Again, use an image your child will understand and relate to.

If your child recognizes some words, you can include these along with the pictures, but keep the descriptions short and use only words they're familiar with. For example, a child might recognize "toys in box" or "wash hands" for a task and "read book" or "go to park" for a reward. If so, write these words or phrases on the contract.

Review the contract together. Use clear language and examples to describe each part of the contract. In "The Pet Menace," Maya's mother took her daughter's hand, pointed to each picture, and explained what each one meant. For the task, she said, "See how the girl is playing nicely with her dog?"

Tip for Success: Keep the task simple for the first contract and make earning the reward very likely. Praise your child for attempting the task and celebrate when they earn the reward. Children who experience success and enjoy their first contract will be more open to using contracts for more challenging tasks in the future.

Demonstrate and role-play the task. Maya's mother showed her daughter what doing the task looked like. "See, Maya, how I'm petting Bella gently? No hitting. And I'm not touching her ears or tail. You try it now." Then she had Maya do it.

Describe or demonstrate the reward. If possible, show the actual reward or provide it after your child has role-played doing the task, for example, reading a story to Maya.

Sign the contract. Once you feel that your child clearly understands each element of the contract, have your child sign their name and watch as you sign yours. If your child cannot sign their name, have your child watch as you sign the contract. Then write their name and have them circle it, or simply have your child make a mark like an X or a squiggle in the spot for their signature.

Add your family's official seal. Pick something meaningful to your family that can be easily duplicated and used consistently. A sheet of stickers that are all the same is an easy way to do this. A family member can also design and draw the official seal, or download and print an image.

Put the contract in a visible place as a reminder. Maya's family taped her Be Nice to the Pets contract on the fish tank. Other typical places to display contracts are on the refrigerator, bathroom mirror, or bedroom door. If you or your child prefers to keep the contract in a more private place, that's fine, too.

HOW TO MAKE A CONTRACT

Select the task

Choose the reward

Write the contract

Implement the contract

If your child isn't interested in contracting at first, don't give up too quickly.

IN THIS CHAPTER, YOU'LL LEARN:

- What you can do if your child doesn't want a contract

16

If Your Child Won't Try Contracting

After reading the *Let's Make a Contract* stories alone or with their parents, many kids are open to trying a contract. Some are even eager to have a contract. But some children remain unimpressed or even hostile toward the idea. Other children aren't opposed to contracting itself but are uncomfortable with any change to their routine.

If your child says no to contracting for any reason, don't argue or try to force them to try it. Arguing will backfire, coercion won't work, and both are contrary to contracting's purpose and positive approach. That doesn't mean you should give up, though. Many parents have found one or a combination of the following strategies an effective way to persuade their children to give contracting a try.

Ignore the Negative and Acknowledge the Positive

Child behavior that receives attention—positive or negative—from you is more likely to continue than behavior that's ignored or downplayed. If your child isn't interested in trying a contract, minimize your reactions to anti-contracting protests and keep any response as neutral as possible. Instead, look for, acknowledge, and praise any, even if slight, positive responses to contracting.

If your child says: "Contracts are stupid," "You'll never get me to sign a contract," or "Don't talk to me about those dumb contracts," stay calm and resist the impulse to try to convince them that contracts are great. For some kids, few things are more rewarding than involving their parents in a lively argument. Instead, respond with a brief neutral statement such as, "I can see you're not interested in trying a contract right now," or "Okay, I hear you."

On the other hand, be ready to respond positively if your child makes any remotely positive, or even neutral, response to the idea of trying contracting, such as picking up this book, looking at another family member's contract, or saying something like: "I wonder if anybody has ever made a contract for . . . ?"

Demonstrate a Contract with a Sibling or Partner

Seeing a successful contract in action might change your reluctant child into an "I'm willing to try it" kid. In families with more than one child, parents can make contracts with a sibling and give them lots of praise for trying the process as well as positive attention for achieving successes.

If your child is an only child and two adults are in the household, make a contract between yourselves to model contracting for your child. If you're a single parent, make a contract with a friend or family member. Do your best to make contracting look fun. Kids who continually see their siblings or parents enjoying contracting might decide to give it a try, too.

If your child decides to try a contract, be careful not to turn it into an "I told you so" situation. A "Welcome aboard! What do you want your first contract to be?" approach will be more effective and consistent with the spirit of keeping the process positive.

Put Your Child in Control of a Reward You Must Earn

Some children are wary of what their parents have in store for them, especially if past interactions have involved negative consequences such as scolding, punishment, or disapproval in response to their behavior. In such cases, the following approach might help.

Say to your child, "Okay, if you don't think contracts are fair [can work, are a good idea, are too much of a change, or whatever your child doesn't like about contracts], let's make a contract for me." Let your child control the reward on a contract specifying a task that you must complete. In this way, your child gets a chance to experience some control in a situation where they might feel powerless.

After participating in a contract calling for their parent to do a task, many kids learn that contracts can be fair, work, and even be fun. At that point, you can suggest turning the tables and initiate a contract specifying a task for your child to complete.

Propose a Self-Contract

Some kids don't believe a contract will be honest. Perhaps your child suspects that when they complete the task, they won't get the reward. A method for dealing with this wariness is to let your child develop and implement a self-contract. Show your child how they can completely control both the task *and* the reward sections of the contract. Perry's self-contract in "The Number Problem" illustrates this approach.

At this point, you might think that kids will choose the easiest task and biggest reward, but counterintuitively, most won't. In fact, research shows that when children are allowed to set their own standards of work and reward, they are sometimes tougher on themselves than when adults set the standards for them.

How to Respond to "I Don't Need a Contract"

Your child might resist contracting by claiming, "I don't need a contract to do those things." Although you feel otherwise—"those things" haven't been getting done without a contract—this may be the time to take your child at their word and see what happens. Say, "All right, let's see if you can do it without a contract."

Even without a contract, you can track your child's progress using a task record form. Make a simple chart or checklist where you or your child records each time they complete the task. You can also use a wall calendar where you place a sticker or draw a mark, such as a star or smiley face, on each day that your child completes the task. Display the task record near where the task occurs; in another visible space, like on the refrigerator; or in a private space your child has easy access to.

If your child does the task consistently without a contract, praise them and celebrate. Simply tracking task completions and giving positive attention to your child's success might be enough to motivate your child.

Tip for Success: If your child still refuses to try contracting after all your efforts, that's okay. As we said at the start of this book, contracting isn't the answer to all problems. Sometimes, other positive parenting approaches will work better. In Resources, we identify several excellent books on evidence-based techniques for improving children's behavior and family relationships.

Glossary

Applied behavior analysis (ABA) A science devoted to understanding and improving human behavior. See References for more information.

Autism, or autism spectrum disorder (ASD) A developmental disability characterized by persistent challenges in communication and social interaction and by restricted, repetitive, and stereotypic patterns of behavior, interests, and activities.

Behavior Any action a person does that can be observed and measured.

Behavior analyst A trained and certified professional who uses applied behavior analysis to help people change their behavior. A registry of Board Certified Behavior Analysts (BCBAs) is available at bacb.com.

Contract A written agreement specifying a task to be performed and a reward to be received after completion of the task (also called *behavior contract* or *contingency contract*).

Contracting A teaching strategy that targets a specific task to be done and a reward that follows successful completion of the task.

If-then relationship The relationship between the task and the reward on a contract; *if* the task is completed, *then* the reward will follow.

My Rewards form A form for identifying possible rewards for contracts. The child and/or a parent lists activities, items, or special treats they might want to as rewards.

My Tasks form A form for identifying possible tasks for contracts. The child and/or a parent lists behaviors they currently do to help the family and other ways they could help the family or themselves in the future.

Official seal A small image a family creates or picks to reflect its identity. When placed on a contract, this personal seal of approval signifies the contract's importance to all the family members who sign the contract.

Picture contract A contract that represents the task and reward with illustrations, photos, and/or symbols.

Replacement behavior A desirable behavior selected to take the place of an inappropriate or challenging behavior.

Reward A positive consequence (for example, a desired item, activity, or privilege) received after completing a task.

Reward menu A list of rewards a person can choose from after successfully completing a contract task.

Self-contract A contract a person makes with themselves by choosing the task and the reward.

Task The behavior a person must do to earn the reward on the contract.

Task Record The part of a contract that visually tracks task completion.

Visual activity schedule A set of illustrations, photos, and/or symbols showing the sequence of activities for a daily routine (for example, getting ready for school) or steps for completing a single task (for example, making a bed). See Resources for more information.

Your Tasks form A form for identifying possible tasks for other family members' contracts.

Resources

Books and Articles for Parents

Barbera, M. L. (2021). *Turn Autism Around: An Action Guide for Parents of Young Children with Early Signs of Autism.* Hay House.

Daniels, A. (2016). *Bringing Out the Best in People: How to Apply the Astonishing Power of Positive Reinforcement* (3rd ed.). McGraw-Hill Education.

Friman, P. C. (2005). *Good Night, Sweet Dreams, I Love You: Now Get Into Bed and Go to Sleep!* Boys Town Press.

Kazdin, A. (2010). "Tiny Tyrants: How to Really Change Your Kid's Behavior." https://slate.com/human-interest/2008/04/how-to-really-change-your-kid-s-behavior.html.

Kazdin, A. E. (2014). *The Everyday Parenting Toolkit: The Kazdin Method for Easy, Step-by-Step, Lasting Change for You and Your Child.* Mariner Books.

Kazdin, A., & Rotella, C. (2010). "If You're Good, I'll Buy You a Toy: The difference between bribing your child and rewarding your child." https://slate.com/human-interest/2010/03/why-bribing-your-child-doesn-t-work.html.

Latham, G. I. (1996). *The Power of Positive Parenting: A Wonderful Way to Raise Children.* P&T Ink.

Maurice, C. (1993). *Let Me Hear Your Voice: A Family's Triumph Over Autism.* Knopf.

Maurice, C., Green, G., & Luce, S. C. (Eds.). (1996). *Behavioral Intervention for Young Children with Autism: A Manual for Parents and Professionals.* Pro-Ed.

Ryan Gregory, C. (2021, April). "9 Special Education Strategies That Work for All Kids." https://www.parents.com/kids/development/behavioral/special-education-strategies-that-work-for-all-kids.

Sounders, B. (2021). "Parenting Children with Positive Reinforcement." https://positivepsychology.com/parenting-positive-reinforcement.

Thompson, T. (2009). *Freedom from Meltdowns: Dr. Thompson's Solution for Children with Autism.* Brookes Publishing.

Online Parenting Course

Everyday Parenting: The ABCs of Child Rearing. This free course taught by Alan Kazdin, Ph.D., ABPP, through Yale University teaches techniques to develop the behaviors you would like to see in your child. https://www.coursera.org/learn/everyday-parenting.

Contracting Resources, Visual Supports, and Apps

Aspen, A., & Stack. L. (2019). "Visual Activity Schedules for Students with Autism Spectrum Disorder." https://www.youtube.com/watch?v=YNfnuuATlkA.

Cohen, M. J., & Gerhardt, P. F. (2015). *Visual Supports for People with Autism: A Guide for Parents and Professionals* (2nd ed.). Woodbine House.

Happy Kids Timer Family Chores. This free visual countdown timer app encourages kids to complete morning and evening routines and be independent.

I-Connect Self-Monitoring. A free app developed at University of Kansas, the I-Connect app is completely customizable and can be set up for virtual learning time, chore time, and even free time. https://iconnect.ku.edu/i-connectathome.

McClannahan, L. E., & Krantz, P. J. (2010). *Activity Schedules for Children with Autism: Teaching Independent Behavior* (2nd ed.). Woodbine House.

PBIS World. (2021). *Behavior Contract.* http://www.pbisworld.com/tier-2/behavior-contract [includes links to a wide variety of contracting resources and forms].

References

Research on Behavior Contracting

Bowman-Perrott, L. D., Burke, M. D., deMarin, S., Zhang, N., & Davis, H. (2015). "A Meta-Analysis of Single-Case Research on Behavior Contracts: Effects on Behavioral and Academic Outcomes among Children and Youth." *Behavior Modification, 39*(2), 247–269.

Gurrad, A. M., Weber, K. P., & McLaughlin, T. F. (2002). "The Effects of Contingency Contracting for a Middle School Student with Attention Deficit Hyperactivity Disorder During Corrective Reading Lessons: A Case Report." *International Journal of Special Education, 17,* 26–31.

Hawkins, E., Kingsdorf, S., Charnock, J., Szabo, M., Middleton, E., Phillips, J., & Gautreaux, G. (2011). "Using Behavior Contracts to Decrease Antisocial Behavior in Four Boys with Autistic Spectrum Disorder at Home and at School." *British Journal of Special Education, 38,* 202–208.

Miller, D.L., & Kelley, M.L. (1994). "The Use of Goal Setting and Contingency Contracting for Improving Children's Homework Performance." *Journal of Applied Behavior Analysis, 27,* 73–84.

Mruzek, D. W., Cohen, C., & Smith, T. (2007). "Contingency Contracting with Students with Autism Spectrum Disorders in a Public School Setting." *Journal of Developmental and Physical Disabilities, 19,* 103–114.

Ruth, W.J. (1996). "Goal Setting and Behavioral Contracting for Students with Emotional and Behavioral Difficulties: Analysis of Daily, Weekly, and Total Goal Attainment." *Psychology in the Schools, 33,* 153–158.

Research on the "Sign Here" Contracting Method

Kabler, M. L. (1976). "Teaching Fourth-Grade Children to Use Self-Contracting as a Form of Self-Control" (Doctoral dissertation). Retrieved from ProQuest Dissertations Publishing, 7702427. [Three fourth-grade teachers used the book *Sign Here* to teach contracting skills to their students.]

Norman, J. E. (1977). "The Effects of Programmed Instructional Materials: Parent Training in Contingency Contracting" (Doctoral dissertation). Retrieved from ProQuest Dissertations Publishing, 7805898. [Parents of children who exhibited persistent behavior problems used the book *Sign Here* to write and implement family contracts. Eight of the nine contracts greatly reduced disruptions in the home.]

Shrewsberry, R. D. (1977). "Assignment Completion in Group Parent Training" (Doctoral dissertation). Retrieved from ProQuest Dissertations Publishing, 7731977. [Fifty-nine families wrote and implemented 154 contracts with their children. The parents judged 138 (90%) of those contracts as successfully increasing completion of the specified task.]

Applied Behavior Analysis: The Science Behind Contracting

Cooper, J. O., Heron, T. E., & Heward, W. L. (2020). *Applied Behavior Analysis* (3rd ed.). Pearson.

Effects of Praise on Children's Behavior

We had never seen such power! The speed and magnitude of the effects on children's behavior in the real world of simple adjustments of something so ubiquitous as adult attention was astounding. Forty years later, social reinforcement (positive attention, praise, "catching them being good") has become the core of most American advice and training for parents and teachers—making this arguably the most influential discovery of modern psychology. —Todd R. Risley (Journal of Applied Behavior Analysis, 2005, p. 280).

Marchant, M., Young, K. R., & West, R. P. (2004). "The Effects of Parental Teaching on Compliance Behavior of Children." *Psychology in the Schools, 41*(3), 337-350.

Moore, T. C., Maggin, D. M., Thompson, K. M., Gordon, J. R., Daniels, S., & Lang, L. E. (2019). "Evidence Review for Teacher Praise to Improve Students' Classroom Behavior." *Journal of Positive Behavior Interventions, 21*(1), 3–18.

Strain, P. S., & Joseph, G. E. (2004). "A Not So Good Job with 'Good job.' " *Journal of Positive Behavior Interventions, 6*(1), 55–59.

Acknowledgments

We are especially indebted to Richard Malott, Ph.D., and Donald Whaley, Ph.D., who thought our proposal to bring contracting to families by way of children's stories merited support. Psychology courses at Western Michigan University taught by these two pioneers in applying behavior science to improving people's lives introduced Bill to behavior analysis as an undergraduate student. *Sign Here,* the forerunner of this book, was published by Malott and Whaley's company Behaviordelia. Walter Barbe, Ph.D., who at the time was Editor-in-Chief of *Highlights for Children*, gave us valuable advice for making the stories interesting to children and their parents and wrote the foreword for the original book.

We thank Michael Kabler, Ph.D., James Norman, Ph.D., and Robert Shrewsberry, Ph.D., whose doctoral dissertations contributed to the research and development of our contracting method using *Sign Here.*

We are grateful to the many people and organizations that have translated and published *Sign Here* to make it available to families all over the world. More details about these translations can be found on page 208. Our global partners include: Nikolay Alipov, Ph.D. (Pirogov Russian National Research Medical University, Moscow); Esteban Armendariz and Fernando Armendariz, Ph.D., BCBA-D (Walden Center, Hermosillo, Mexico); Anca Dumitrescu, BCBA (Autism Voice, Bucharest, Romania), Giovanni Maria Guazzo, PsyD., Senior Behavior Analyst (University of Salerno, Salerno, Italy); Yini Liao, Ph.D., BCBA

(Sun Yat-sen University, Guangzhou, China); Kathryn Mendoza, BCBA, and Ian Russel Mendoza (ABA Training Solutions, Manilla, Philippines); Karel Pancocha, Ph.D., BCBA (Masaryk University, Brno, Czech Republic); Marta Sierocka-Rogala, BCBA (Fundacja Scolaris, Warsaw, Poland); Ayako Tamura (manga author/artist, Hakodate, Japan); Sakurako Tanaka, Ph.D., BCBA-D (Asia-Pacific ABA Network); and Li Wu (Trinity College Dublin, Ireland).

Transforming *Sign Here* into *Let's Make a Contract* has been a team effort. A shout-out to Kimberly Nix Berens, Ph.D., author of *Blind Spots: Why Students Fail and the Science That Can Save Them*, for introducing us to The Collective Book Studio. Founder Angela Engel and acquisitions editor Elisabeth Saake have an infectious passion for making books that matter. Designer David Miles and illustrator Albert Pinilla turned our text into this beautiful book. Copyeditors Meg Dendler and Tamar Schwartz gave our manuscript a final tune-up.

Developmental editor Elizabeth Dougherty provided encouragement, enthusiasm, and guidance. Elizabeth's editorial expertise is apparent on every page. She was a delight to work with. We will miss our weekly "Zooms with Zed."

Moira Konrad, Ph.D., our excellent beta reader, provided many spot-on suggestions that we incorporated into the manuscript.

We are especially grateful to Catherine Maurice for her ongoing support and encouragement. Her powerful book, *Let Me Hear Your Voice,* continues to inform parents around the world of the effectiveness of education and treatment based on ABA for children with autism.

Finally, and most of all, we thank the families we've been privileged to work with and learn from over the years. Their experiences and insights taught us valuable lessons we're pleased to share with you through this book.

Contract Forms

CONTRACT

TASK

* Who:

* What:

* When:

* How well:

REWARD

* Who:

* What:

* When:

* How much:

M	T	W	Th	F	M	T	W	Th	F	M	T	W	Th	F

Sign here: _____ _____

Sign here: _____ _____

CONTRACT

TASK	REWARD
* Who:	* Who:
* What:	* What:
* When:	* When:
* How well:	* How much:

Sign here: _____

Sign here: _____

CONTRACT

TASK

* Who:

* What:

* When:

* How well:

REWARD

* Who:

* What:

* When:

* How much:

Sign here: _____

Sign here: _____

S	M	T	W	Th	F	Sat	S	M	T	W	Th	F	Sat	S	M	T	W	Th	F	Sat

MY TASKS:

THINGS I DO TO HELP MY FAMILY	OTHER WAYS I COULD HELP MY FAMILY AND MYSELF
•	•
•	•
•	•
•	•
•	•
•	•
•	•
•	•
•	•
•	•

YOUR TASKS:

WHAT	OTHER WAYS
DOES TO HELP OUR FAMILY	COULD HELP
•	•
•	•
•	•
•	•
•	•
•	•
•	•
•	•
•	•

MY REWARDS:

AT-HOME ACTIVITIES

-
-
-
-

SPECIAL TREATS/ITEMS

-
-
-
-

COMMUNITY ACTIVITIES

-
-
-
-

OTHER

-
-
-
-

MY REWARDS:

MY FAVORITE ACTIVITIES, THINGS, AND SPECIAL TREATS

-
-
-
-
-
-
-
-
-
-
-
-
-
-

Translations

Translations of an earlier version of *Let's Make a Contract* (titled *Sign Here: A Contracting Book for Children and Their Parents*, 2nd Edition) include:

- Chinese (2021). Sun Yat-sen University Press. www.zsup.com.cn
- Czech (2018). Masaryk University Press. www.muni.cz/pro-media/tiskove-zpravy/ pedagogove-vydali-knihu-o-smlouvani-mezi-rodici-a-detmi
- Filipino (2022). ABA Training Solutions.
- Italian (2017). Institute for Research, Training and Information on Disabilities. www.libreriauniversitaria.it/ firma-qui-libro-contratti-educativi/libro/9788894155211
- Japanese (2022). Tokyo: Akashi-Shoten.
- Polish (2017). Fundacja Scolaris. https://kropka-sklep.pl/produkt/ umowmy-sie/
- Romanian (2016). Autism Voice. https://shop.autismvoice.ro/carti/26-cartea-semneaza-aici.html
- Russian (2016). Practica Publishing. www.practica.ru/catalogue/ davai-dogovorimsia_272/
- Spanish (2020). Walden Center, Hermosillo, Mexico.
- Turkish (2018). Tohum Autism Foundation. www.nobelkitap.com/ buraya-imzanizi-atiniz-386798.html